# The Perfect Dozen

*Jake with his brood. Tobey and Dixie stand out beside him.*

# The Perfect Dozen

by Gail Nelson Canada

*For Lee, thank you
for Reading our Story
and for loving our
4-legged friends —
Gail Nelson Canada*

**BELLE ISLE BOOKS**
www.belleislebooks.com

Printed in the United States

ISBN: 9781939930620

Library of Congress Control Number: 2015954522

BELLE ISLE BOOKS

www.belleislebooks.com

This book is dedicated to all the people who love their pets like family, who have experienced the joy they bring into our lives, and felt the tremendous grief in the loss of one.
In particular, it is dedicated to the wonderful people who adopted Jake and Hannah's puppies and have given them the loving homes I had hoped they would have.
Thank you.

# CONTENTS

# Prologue
## *Dixie*
### The Reason to Write

It's August 5, 2013. I'm sitting on our deck with my baby girl, Dixie Doodle. It's a beautiful summer day and Dixie is lying beside my deck chair, the sun warming her coat. She has such a thick, silky coat, so soft. None of the other pups inherited such a luxurious outer covering. Tobey knows that I am upset and has come up the deck steps to check on me. He puts his head on my knee and looks up at me as if to say everything will be all right. My hero: he always seems worried if I'm not feeling well or am upset. Dixie is happy—she doesn't know how sick she is—and I can't seem to stop crying.

We've just returned from the oncologist. The X-rays taken today showed that the cancer has moved to the lungs—not just a few lesions, but all over the lungs. It happened so fast. She's had blood-work done every week and all the results had always been good. Until they weren't. Now we're left with the option of doing an expensive chemotherapy treatment (as if the other ones hadn't been inexpensive), a type of inhalant with a 30 percent chance of working. Though the oncologist has never seen it actually eliminate a case of cancer, there are records of it alleviating cancer in dogs with just a few lesions; but not as many as Dixie has.

They said she has a very aggressive cancer. The other three chemo treatments—two for the osteosarcoma and one that was supposed to be effective against melanoma as well as another type of cancer that affects the blood—didn't work. She still has a tumor that has not decreased in size above her amputated leg. Now that it's spread to her lungs, there's not much hope of curing her. The doctors prescribed antibiotics and prednisone. The prednisone is supposed to help decrease her tumors and increase her appetite; the antibiotics are in case she winds up with an infection from the lung lesions. Now, we have to wean her off the Novox, a drug used for inflammation and pain, for five days before we can give her the prednisone. We may have two more months with her. We had such high hopes of keeping her with us a lot longer.

I don't have children of my own; these puppies are like my children. The pain of watching one of them suffer an incurable disease, of sitting by and witnessing her deterioration, is just unbearable. You expect to outlive your pets, but you also expect to have them longer than five and a half years. I can't even talk to anyone about it without breaking down in agonizing sobs.

I saw a couple's story on TV recently. They had a young son— he may have been two—who had incurable leukemia and was only expected to live another two months. They were not married yet, but were planning their wedding and decided to push their wedding date up. Family and friends helped to put it together for them so that their son could be the best man at the ceremony. So sweet. It's odd to feel a connection with that couple, but I do. I'm so scared to watch Dixie suffer.

# 1

## *Jake*

### The Beginning

This story begins back in the summer of 1997. It was my habit to exercise by running from our house, nestled in the woods on the back part of our family farm, to the paved road, taking a left, and then running across the creek that was the Chesterfield county line. Round-trip past a few neighbors' houses was about four miles.

It was a warm morning when a black Lab puppy appeared, running on the road as well. He seemed quite lost, and began following me (my husband says I coaxed him) all the way home. The poor boy had ticks all over him from roaming the nearby woods. He seemed to enjoy the insecticide bath as well as the attention I gave him. It looked like he had worn a collar recently, because the hair was matted down around his neck. Whoever dropped him off must have decided they didn't want to be contacted; there was no collar or name tag. A lot of ignorant people think it's better to drop a dog or cat off in the country—like they can take care of themselves!—where they could starve or get hit by a car, than it is to take them to a no-kill humane shelter where they would at least have a chance of being adopted.

He was an affectionate puppy, but awfully clumsy, with the biggest paws I had ever seen. Unlike most pups, he didn't seem to know how to play, and he was afraid of the flyswatter and the sound of aluminum foil; he would hide under the table at those sounds. It was almost like someone had kept him confined to a crate in an apartment until he got too big. I can't imagine how anyone could be mean to such a sweet boy.

He was only five months old, and weighed in at fifty-three pounds. We could tell he was purebred, because he looked identical to a purebred English Lab a friend of ours had. Our friend said it was just a shame the people who dumped him off on the side of the road hadn't bothered to tie his papers around his neck. We named him Jake.

As time went on, Jake kept growing bigger and bigger. At three years old, he weighed in at 121 pounds. At six years old, he was a whopping 146.2 pounds. He was very active as a pup, bounding through the woods like a deer, and he would jump straight up like a kangaroo when he got excited. He also loved to chase squirrels and would practically climb a tree to get at one. He never caught one, but many times he came close.

*Young Jake treeing a squirrel, with Muffin as his sidekick.*

My father gave me land to build on before he passed away (this was a common practice for farmers), and I chose a twenty-acre parcel a half-mile from the hard-surface road, so we didn't have to worry much about Jake straying. He seemed content to stay close to us. Our other dogs at the time—Muffin, a rescued beagle; and Dillon, a Chesapeake Lab mix who looked more like a bear—kept Jake company when we weren't home.

Hunting season starts in November, and at almost a year old, Jake had a strong inclination to chase any animal through the woods, deer being a favorite. I was afraid he'd run after a deer and get shot by mistake or get lost, unable to find his way back home. He would start chasing a deer, and you'd call him and call him, but he wouldn't listen and wouldn't come back until he got tired. So we thought an invisible fence would be the best solution.

We bought the fence from Lowe's and installed it ourselves. It wasn't terribly expensive and, naturally, didn't create an eyesore around our property. My husband Randy is so smart. He put a metal pipe under the driveway to run the wire through, so it wouldn't get broken by vehicles coming or going. Jake had about two acres in which to run around the house without crossing the line. There was, of course, significant training involved; the fence came with written instructions and a video. It also came with these white flags on wire posts that you stuck in the ground around the whole perimeter, just inside the invisible fence wire. We would take Jake out into the yard and show him the flags, tell him "no," shake the flag, and then walk him around the two-acre perimeter, repeating this instruction every six to ten flags. The whole process took about forty-five minutes, and this training was to be repeated every day for two weeks, once in the a.m. and once in the p.m. If you're familiar with hunting season, you know the weather can sometimes be iffy—cold and rainy usually—but nonetheless we were diligent, and at the end of the two weeks, we felt confident he was trained. It was time to test it.

We secured the shock collar around Jake's neck and led him outside. Within seconds, he spotted a squirrel, and promptly through the fence he went. The squirrel got away, but rather than return to us, Jake sat on the other side of the fence, knowing he would get shocked coming back into the yard. He patiently waited for us to retrieve him, take his shock collar off, and walk him back behind safe lines. We repeated this routine several times. Then we found out there was a nine-volt "stubborn" dog collar. We purchased it as soon as possible. After we switched his collar, he went through the fence one time and decided not to do that again. Labs are quick learners.

Jake was such a sweet boy, so smart and sensitive. For instance, one time my sister visited us with her Maltese puppy, Angel. Angel would sit on the arm of the sofa, next to my sister, feeling

*Patient Jake, not sure about the cowgirl!*

confident in her status, as three-pound lap dogs do. Jake became curious about this little white fluffball and went over to investigate. She immediately snapped at him. His feelings were so hurt, he slumped off with his tail between his legs. She eventually warmed up to him, but he kept his distance, afraid she might snap at him again.

Jake loved sleeping in the bed with us and knew when it was time to go to bed. If we were watching a movie and it was getting close to bedtime, he would come and stand in front of us, staring. If we didn't get up to go to bed, he just went on without us. Sometimes, it could be a struggle finding a spot for ourselves in that bed.

## 2

## *Hannah*

By he summer of 2003, Jake was seven years old, and the time for him to produce puppies was growing limited. We (or maybe it was just me) decided we needed Jake puppies. I wouldn't know how to handle losing him without keeping a part of him with us. So I searched the classifieds, found a litter of yellow Lab pups for sale, and Randy and I made an appointment to see the pups. We found it refreshing that the owners weren't "true" breeders who were more concerned about making money than the well-being of their pets. They had a sweet momma dog and had fixed their garage to accommodate her new litter. The couple made sure the space was always clean, and you could tell they loved their girl.

In that garage were seven of the cutest puppies we had ever seen. It was so hard to choose. We picked out three and had them run around the garage as we tried to choose our new baby girl. We wanted to make sure that she would grow up to be a big Lab, since Jake was so big. We really liked the box-head of the English Lab and their large size. The owners showed us photos of the puppies' father, who was large in stature and had that pretty head. Their mom was large for a Lab as well. Their impressive pedigree showed that they had American Labs and English Labs in their background.

Eventually, Randy chose Hannah because she was one of the largest and had the biggest paws. I agreed. Then the owners informed us that someone else had already put a $200 deposit down (the sale price was $800) on Hannah, and they would have to let us know whether she could be ours. She was six weeks old and even if the other sale fell through, we wouldn't be able take her home until she was eight weeks old. That meant two weeks of anticipation. We didn't want to leave her.

Then, just a few days after our visit, we got a phone call from the breeder. We were overjoyed to learn that the lady who had made the deposit couldn't take the pup, and had generously applied the $200 toward our purchase of Hannah. Even with that $200, Randy still couldn't believe we were paying $600 for a puppy! But she was worth every cent!

Hannah was born on June 29, 2003, and we brought her home in August. She was and still is such a doll-baby. She loves to play ball and loves the water. Since it was still summer and hot, we bought her a hard plastic kiddie pool to play in. She loved it! We'd throw the ball in the water and she would actually put her head under the water to retrieve it; we had never seen that before. Jake enjoyed the kiddie pool, too, but he would just lie down in it to chill, taking up the entire width of the pool.

Our hope was that Hannah and Jake would just naturally make puppies, preferably after she was at least a year old. Females come into heat every six months, and it was a demanding task keeping Jake away from her until she was of age. When Hannah first came into heat, we made Jake sleep in the basement at night, while Hannah slept in our bed.

Female dogs in heat are a bit messy, and there is cleanup involved. Someone came up with a wonderful invention called doggy panties for such instances, and when Hannah was in the house, she had on the cutest plaid panties with Velcro attachments. Normally, Randy and I had to work during the day, so Hannah stayed in the outdoor pen with Jake standing guard outside.

One afternoon, after arriving home from work, I went to let Hannah out of her pen, but she was nowhere to be seen. She had gotten out somehow (magically!). Searching frantically, I found her and Jake in the basement, panting as if they were worn out. I panicked and called my cousin, Dr. Bill. We are so blessed to have him as our veterinarian. He is very generous with his time and has helped us by phone whenever we've needed his advice. He informed me that there was nothing we could do but wait.

It turned out Jake was panting because he was so tired from trying to get Hannah pregnant. Come to find out, "Miss Priss" would just sit down, and though Jake would try his best, she was obstinate and he couldn't have his way with her.

In September of 2005, we were fortunate (or maybe not so fortunate) to buy a beach house on Topsail Island. We fell in love with Topsail and had been looking for an investment that we could upgrade, sell, or rent and make a few dollars on. The house wasn't oceanfront, but it was a short walk from the beach, totally furnished, and newly renovated, and, we hoped at the time, rentable. Renting it has worked out so far, but the market crashed, and if we don't win the lottery, we'll have to sell.

Anyway, Jake and Hannah had never been to the beach, and this beach was extremely dog friendly. There were even doggy stations with plastic bags at every beach access point so people who walked their dogs on the beach could clean up after them. No bombs on that beach!

It was late spring when we took the dogs to the new house to experience the beach. We found that Hannah was such a "nervous Nellie," she would stand up in the truck the whole way down, a four-and-a-half-hour drive. She was too nervous to lie down. Jake, on the other hand, has always been so laid-back; he enjoyed the ride and the attention.

*Jake and Hannah's first beach trip*

In early spring, there was no leash law on the beach, and very few people, so the dogs got to explore and enjoy the waves with no limitations. Hannah was a bit shocked by the taste of salt water. She did not like it at first, but the motivation of fetching the ball we'd throw into the waves overrode the bad taste, and she was after that ball continuously. It was impossible to wear her out. She loved retrieving the ball from the waves and was so anxious to get to the beach that she would pull us along the highway, fighting the leash and choking all the way. We had not done a good job leash training her. As for Jake, he loved to just explore and lie on the beach, letting the waves roll under him.

Jake had been having trouble with his back hurting, and had begun walking a bit like John Wayne. We hadn't watched his weight like we should have, and the extra weight and age made it painful for him to walk up flights of stairs. We now had to pick him up to put him in the bed at night. He'd put his front feet on the bed and wait for us to lift him the rest of the way. When he was younger he would just jump up on the bed to sleep with us. Jake did really well on this trip; all our extra attention just made him feel special, which he was.

Since we planned to rent the house to vacationers, we kept the dogs on the top floor to cut down on cleaning. It was amazing that we still found dog hair hiding in the most unusual places two to three months later. Labs do have a tendency to shed year-round. We are such sticklers about the house being clean for renters that we have not taken them back. But it was so much fun that we may take Hannah and the pups back for their beach experience or rent somewhere else that allows dogs on the beach in the future.

Exercise is so important to dogs, especially Labs. Jake and Hannah would go for excursions to the lake, or hiking in the mountains, or just on trips to the hay fields to play ball and sniff around. Our Dodge van, which used to be my work truck, is now the dog truck. The side doors make it easy for the dogs to jump into and out of the truck, and it's so open that they can easily climb onto the front seats to look out the windows.

*Jake and Hannah chasing new scents near the pond*

*Majestic Jake at peak weight*

During September and October of 2006, Jake started losing weight and drinking a lot of water. He acted like he wasn't feeling well. At first I gave him pain medication, thinking his back was hurting him. But when his appetite decreased, I was concerned. He had always been one to eat anything and everything.

One morning, Jake was headed outside as usual and threw up blood before he even made it out of the bedroom. I immediately called Bill and took Jake into the clinic. Bill kept him overnight, doing extensive blood tests and giving him IVs. His tests showed that Jake was diabetic and possibly had bleeding ulcers. He recommended an ultrasound and some other tests and suggested that we take him to the emergency clinic for twenty-four-hour care. Of course, these things always seem to happen on or right before the weekend.

The emergency clinic kept him for two nights as well. We were able to visit Jake at both clinics, so he wouldn't feel alone in an unfamiliar place with unfamiliar people. They treated his ulcers and monitored his insulin levels. Everyone at the clinic loved Jake, but he was glad to come home. We were just glad he was going to be all right. We learned how to give him insulin shots, which had to be administered twice a day. He was so good about it, and it was easy to do, but our life began to revolve around the 7 a.m. and 7 p.m. doses.

We've been blessed with great friends who would house-sit for us if we needed to leave to check on the beach house or just get away for a few days. They learned to give Jake his shots and other medications. He was no trouble at all, and our friends couldn't help but love him too.

# 3

## The Adventure

When Hannah turned four years old and Jake was going on twelve, there were still no puppies. I told Bill we wanted Jake puppies, and he referred us to a canine fertility specialist. What an adventure!

An appointment was made to see if Jake was capable of impregnating Hannah. Because of his age, it was questionable. The test they performed was something else. To collect a sample, the veterinarian had to massage Jake and gather his sperm in a rubber sleeve. Jake didn't have a clue what was going on; he was still a virgin. Afterward, my husband liked to joke that on our third appointment to visit the fertility clinic, we couldn't find Jake anywhere—then we heard the car horn blowing, and found Jake behind the wheel, anxious to get going!

It turned out that Jake was a viable candidate. So when Hannah came into heat again, I had to take her to the specialty clinic to test her hormone levels every week, sometimes twice a week. I didn't realize that during the three-week menstrual cycle there are only five days when a female dog can get pregnant and the timing has to be just right. Our work schedule revolved around Hannah's doctor visits. All told, it took several weeks and several visits. Finally, they told us she was ready and to bring her in the next two days to be artificially inseminated. They wanted to inseminate her two days in a row since the time window was so small. That was August 15 and 16, 2007.

Once Hannah tested positive for being pregnant, the clinic recommended an ultrasound to see how many puppies we could expect. The ultrasound was conducted by Dr. Bill, and showed seven puppies. That sounded manageable, since an average litter is eight to ten pups.

Hannah grew bigger and bigger, her belly almost dragging on the ground. She and Jake had always slept with us at night in our double bed. After sharing the bed with "big" Hannah, Jake finally decided the floor was easier. Poor Hannah would lie in the bed at night, shaking the bed with her panting. All those puppies!

*Big-belly Hannah*

# 4

## *The Birth*

The due date for "our babies" was getting close, so we tried to think of everything we would need for the new arrivals. Randy had built a birthing box for Hannah at the foot of our bed. It had four sides approximately eight inches tall to keep the babies inside and a twin mattress as its base with a waterproof mattress cover and blankets. There were also plenty of old clean towels ready for cleanup.

On October 15, 2007, Hannah began pacing and panting. Randy and I decided to tag-team that day. I had to work that morning and he had to leave for appointments that afternoon. You know how it is when you feel like something's going to happen. I just knew the puppies were on their way.

Just after I got home, at about three in the afternoon, Hannah started vomiting. I brought her into the house and led her to the bedroom. She wanted to get on our bed, but I made her lie down on the birthing bed. She did as instructed, and about ten minutes later, the first puppy popped out, a black one.

Hannah looked at her posterior and that puppy in total surprise and bewilderment. I had a damp towel ready to clean the pup, and made sure he was able to nurse. It's important for the puppies to drink mother's milk; it has properties they need for their immune system.

About an hour later, the second pup was born, another black one. Then, about thirty minutes later, a yellow one popped out. By this time, Randy had come home to help, and we were so excited! We didn't think we would have any yellow ones, since black is the dominant color in Labs, but we had hoped.

By ten that night, we had eight puppies. By midnight, when the calendar rolled over to October 16, Randy's birthday, we had ten! We decided to take a nap to rest. Randy woke me at 2 a.m.; Hannah was having another pup. I popped up to assist the delivery. Then I tried again to get a little sleep by lying down on the sofa. Randy called for me at 4 a.m.; another pup arrived. We had the perfect dozen: six males, six females; six black, six yellow. Hannah was so tired.

Early the next morning, we packed the brood up in a plastic hamper with towels and took the pups and Hannah to see Dr. Bill. He took one look at Hannah and said he didn't think she was done. An X-ray revealed two pups still in the birth canal. One had been there since 4 or 5 a.m. He gave Hannah a shot to help her

*The first eight: I thought we had a bonus pup.*

*Worn-out Hannah*

bring those pups into the world. About forty-five minutes later, number thirteen came out, a black male. He was a bit lethargic, but breathing, and I rubbed his little body and tried to get him to nurse. I thought he did. Another twenty-five minutes later, number fourteen came out kicking, a little black female.

I took Hannah and her fourteen puppies home. Hannah climbed onto the birthing bed and I positioned all the pups around her, trying to make sure the two newest ones drank mother's milk.

Bill had recommended supplementing Hannah's milk, since she couldn't accommodate fourteen; she only had eight place settings. We purchased baby bottles and puppy formula.

We let Hannah stay in the birthing bed with the puppies that day. She seemed uncomfortable with all those wriggling babies around her. We, of course, went to bed early after such a long night.

At some point during the night, I was awakened by a whimpering sound from under my night table and found a black male, number thirteen, out in the cold. I couldn't figure out how he'd gotten there, so I put him back in the bed with Hannah. A few hours later, the same thing happened: I found him out of the birthing bed.

Sometimes a mother dog senses something is wrong with a pup and will actually pick him up and discard him. I scooped him up and just held him for a while, keeping him warm. About an hour went by, and he suddenly stiffened up like a board. He was having some kind of seizure. I rubbed him with both hands to increase his circulation until he recovered, and seemed all right. Later on that morning, he started having seizures on a regular basis. In a panic, I called Dr. Bill to make an emergency appointment. Randy drove as fast as he could to the clinic without getting a ticket. All the while I was rubbing the little black pup back to normal after each seizure, afraid that he wouldn't make it.

Dr. Bill thought the problem might be a sugar imbalance, since the pup hadn't arrived on time and had been stuck in the birth canal for so long. They kept him all morning and gave him glucose. Bill called around 1 p.m. and said he was doing well enough to come home. I was so excited that I rushed out to pick him up from the clinic. Thinking that I wouldn't be gone long, I left Hannah in the bed with the puppies. On the way, I decided to name puppy thirteen "Lucky."

I brought Lucky home with instructions on how to feed him sugar water through a tube. I carried him in a box with a towel as a bed and took him into the bedroom where Hannah and the other pups were. Checking on the pups, I found a yellow female lifeless. Hannah had lain on her. I did mouth-to-mouth resuscitation, rubbed her chest, and tried everything I could think of to revive her. But it was no use. I was devastated. I should have known better than to leave Hannah in the bed with all those pups. She has always just plopped down, even on top of us, not paying attention to what she was lying on.

Later that afternoon, the tube feeding didn't work for Lucky, and he passed as well. I was a total basket case, calling Randy and sobbing uncontrollably. I laid the pups in a pretty box with a towel, and Randy buried them near the bend in the road beside the driveway. I cried all that night. From then on, we wouldn't leave Hannah alone with the puppies.

Puppies, like any babies, need to eat all the time. If they don't eat every two hours, they'll let you know they're hungry by whimpering or making sucking noises. They will also suckle the closest sibling if their mother isn't around. We became very efficient with fixing formula and feeding two or three pups at a time, since they always seemed to be hungry at the same time. The formula was usually premixed, but we had to heat it and put it into baby bottles. I got so adept at juggling baby bottles that I could feed two at a time all on my own, and Randy was really good at heating the formula and filling bottles.

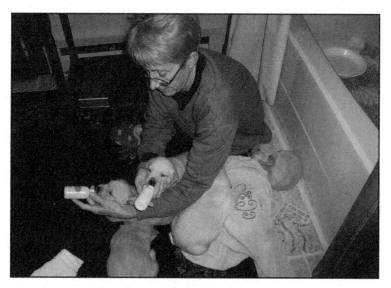

*Two at a time at 2 a.m.*

21

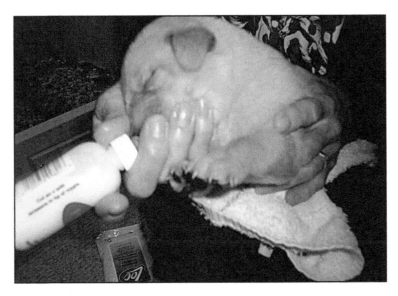

*Dixie with one of her many bottles*

Randy was such a good sport. Feeding them every two hours meant getting up throughout the night. I'd hear them sucking on each other and I'd get up to make formula. He would feed one; I would feed two. Then we'd put the fed ones in a cardboard box with the time of feeding on a sticky note to help us keep up with who had been fed and when. Usually, there were two puppies to a box. We were surprised to learn from Dr. Bill that after feedings, the momma dog would coax the pups to poop by licking them. This duty was now left up to us—not the actual licking; we used a warm washcloth!

We also used the cardboard boxes as "time-out" boxes. (Randy had been after me about keeping all those cardboard boxes around, but I knew they'd come in handy!) I'd wake up from a dead sleep to sucking noises, which meant they were suckling each other when it wasn't time to eat. So we'd put them in time-out boxes to separate the suckers from the non-suckers. The walls of our bedroom were lined with boxes.

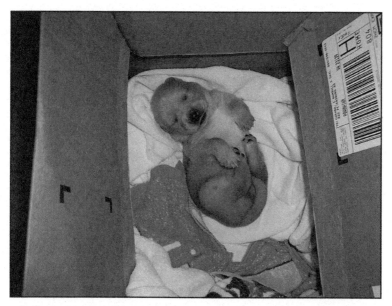

*Dixie lying on her back, sleeping after a bottle, her birthmarks showing—*
*a white spot on forehead and black "z" on her leg.*

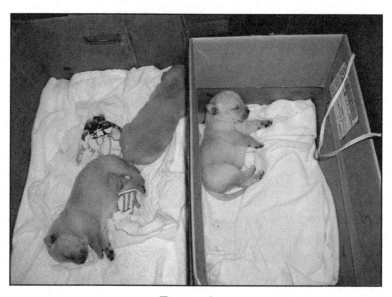

*Time-out boxes*

*Milk makes you sleepy.*

*They loved sleeping on their backs.*

They were all so good and didn't have any problem sucking those bottles empty. I could tell Dixie apart from all the other yellow ones, because she had a white mark in the middle of her forehead and a black "z" mark on her hind leg. Dixie was always the first one to come back for a second bottle. She would push all the others out of the way to get that coveted bottle.

The puppies were just precious. The yellow ones had black paw pads, which seemed so unusual. Jake must have had yellow Labs in his genealogy, because all the yellow ones turned out more like him than the black ones.

*Where's my breakfast? Let me outta here!*

*"Look, Momma, I learned to sit up. Can I have a snack?"*

*"Do you know what Tobey did today?"*

At about four weeks, the puppies graduated to more solid food. It was a kind of mush: a combination of puppy chow and formula. Feeding them in the kiddie pool in the living room seemed like a good way to confine the slop. Of course, baths were required after each feeding.

*Puppies in "slop"*

Jake was good about the new arrivals. He was really curious when they were tiny, but after a while he would try to stay out of the way, acting disinterested. When the pups got big enough to jump out of the box, they would follow him around like he was the momma. When he would lie down, they would lie right next to him or on top of him. He was a good daddy. The puppies just loved him. He wasn't as mobile as he used to be, so he would just plop down and let them lick his mouth or crawl over him.

*Like father, like son*

*Jake look-alikes*

*The world's longest puppy: Dixie and Tobey under the kitchen hutch.*

*Pile of pups with Blake (Randy's daughter) and me in the basement*

By the time the puppies were old enough to graduate to the basement, I had forgotten what a good night's sleep was like. We could still hear them whimpering, whining, or barking, so they'd still wake us up early to have us take care of their needs, whatever those might be.

After five weeks of very little sleep, Randy and I had gotten a bit testy with one another, he more so than me. He said he'd never go through this again, that it was all my idea! It was one of the best experiences of my life and I'd do it again in an instant, but I wouldn't put him through it again.

*The first of many barricades*

*Pups waiting to come inside to get into mischief*

*A lot to explore*

*They loved playing in the leaves, hiding from each other.*

*Dixie and Tobey, side by side*

# 5

## *Puppies at Play*

At five weeks, the pups weighed more than ten pounds each. They were still too little to walk or run up the basement steps by themselves, so we would carry them up the steps to the backyard two at a time for breakfast in the morning, and back down the steps after dinner to sleep at night. I lost several pounds with that workout.

Instead of the kiddie pool, we now used several aluminum turkey pans to feed them, so it took some time to make their meals and have it all ready to go at one time. At this age, we were feeding them three times a day. We'd let them play in the yard until their meals were ready. Then Randy or I would call "PUPPIES!" and they'd all come running, knowing it was time to eat. For the longest time, every one of them thought their name was PUPPIES! Our pups still perk up their ears when they hear that call.

Of course, they still needed a bath after eating, and damp towels were good for cleanup, but they were already outside to do their "business." Now that they were allowed to play in the yard, we had to puppy-proof it for their safety. That took some ingenuity. They could get under and into places we didn't even know about, and they were curious about everything. They would get into situations that they couldn't get out of without help. They found areas under the hot tub platform, back stoop, side deck, and front porch especially interesting, so we had to board up any entry to those dark places because they would invariably get stuck and have to be rescued. We used whatever scrap building materials we could find to shut off such openings. This was not an attractive landscape, but it was functional. We built a barricade in front of the outdoor basement steps to keep them from falling down the stairs when they were playing in the yard. We also secured a tarp over the basement steps in case the pups climbed over the barricades. They seemed to be growing so fast, as all babies do, that we had to increase the height of the barricades routinely. We did that for the birthing bed too, but it didn't take long for them to figure out how to get over it. It was amazing how they could climb and get into stuff. It was also amazing how quick they were.

*Looking for mischief*

We had to keep a close eye on all the pups when they were playing in the yard. Randy would be on the front porch and I would be in the backyard, doing a head count: "I have two yellow and four black in the front!" And I would respond that I had two yellow and three black back here. Oh no! We'd be missing someone and off to find and fetch the scoundrel!

When they were old enough, we bought all the girls tiny pink collars and the boys tiny blue collars. The women who worked at Bill's clinic got a kick out of that. Randy and I had to work together to take the twelve puppies in for their check-up appointments. At first, we'd bring them in two big boxes, but by the time they were six weeks old, they had the run of the back of the Suburban. When we got to the clinic, we had to take them in four at a time. It was amazing what kind of mischief the others could get into in the truck while we were gone for just a few minutes. Wiring was destroyed, papers chewed; and we really worried about the seats! I tried to leave them things like chew bones that would be okay to gnaw; but of course, those were not as interesting as the interior of the truck!

When we went to work in the mornings, we would put the pups in the outdoor kennel, with Mom, Dad, and Muffin watching over them from the yard. We were still feeding them three times a day, so I would usually come home for their lunch and stay with

*All huddled up; must be a bit chilly*

them for the rest of the afternoon. Then, after dinner, we'd carry them down to their basement beds for the night. Many times, we'd go down just to play with them until they went to sleep.

*"Hey, Mom, time for a snack?"*

*Pups and Jake loving on my nephew, Nelson*

As autumn faded into winter, we knew our time with our perfect dozen was growing short. We certainly couldn't keep twelve young Labs in addition to Hannah and Jake. So we made arrangements to find homes for most of the puppies around the holidays. We would keep just two for ourselves. We placed an ad in the paper and let our friends know we had puppies for sale. And so as Christmas neared, one puppy after another was chosen. They would remain with us until they were at least eight weeks old, and then they'd go to their new homes.

I cried after each departure, particularly those of the pups that I might not see again. All the pups' adoptive parents signed an agreement before they took their baby home. They agreed to have a fenced-in yard, whether the fence was invisible or not; to allow visitation from us; and if for any reason they wanted to give the pup up, to bring it back to us.

I kept a puppy book with a page dedicated to each puppy, one through twelve, so I could record the dates of their vet visits, along with their weight, colors, and specific markings. It was with the help of that book and the puppies' owners that I was able to record their stories here.

# 6

## *Puppies 1-12*

### FAITH

Puppy number one was a solid black female. She was originally adopted by a man named David for his girlfriend Janet, who had recently lost a dog. He was so excited and named the puppy "Faith." But just a few days after taking her, he called and told us his girlfriend didn't want the puppy. He was disappointed and upset and said he had tried to figure out a way to keep her himself but couldn't. I really felt bad for him and offered to give him his money back, but he wouldn't take it. Such a sweet man. I hope he's been able to get another pup for himself since then.

*Little girl with proud adopters*

We were still getting calls about our puppy ad. We could have found homes for twelve more pups if we'd had them. Now we had Faith to find another home for. A woman who works with horses adopted her and planned to take her along on farm visits, which sounded like such fun for our pup. Faith was very full of herself. She was climbing over the front seat to explore her new owner's SUV as they drove away down the driveway.

I have thought about doing a puppy reunion every year since their birth, but I was always afraid of hearing bad news. In writing this book, I called all the pups' owners to ask if they would write their pup's story and send us recent photos. The first call I made was to the woman who works with horses, who told us that Faith had been re-named "Tessa" and had passed away from some type of infection a couple of years ago, which would have made her just three years old. When I heard this, my heart dropped to my stomach and tears ran down my face. After that, I was hesitant to call the others, afraid of hearing more bad news. But this book is for my Dixie, and I really wanted to find out about all the pups.

Faith's mom sent me an e-mail to express her sympathy for Dixie's illness, and to opt out of being included in our book. She and her husband are authors and have a contract with a publishing agent, which restricts them from writing in any other publications. They didn't wish to have a photo published either. We understand and respect their wishes, but regret that Faith's story will not be told.

## KIMBER

I was uplifted by my next call.

Puppy number two was a black female with a small streak of white on her chest. Her new owners, Tommy and Anita, named her Kimber. They have two children who adored her and taught her to ride jet skis on the Chesapeake Bay. When I first talked to Anita, she was so excited to tell me about Kimber and how wonderful she was. Kimber was her children's best friend, and it sounded like she had the perfect Lab life.

*Kimber at the water's edge*

*Kimber on a jet ski*

*Kimber riding a tube*

*Baby Kimber with her new best friends*

*Searching for minnows*

*Such a sweet soul (Kimber with kitten)*

Not long after, though, I received a heart-wrenching letter from Anita:

*Gail and Randy,*

*I am typing this with a broken heart. I wanted to call several times but can't even talk about it. We had to put Kimber down on Saturday, December 28th. She had cancer. On Thursday, she stopped eating. Saturday morning she could not even stand on her back legs. I rushed her to an emergency vet and after several tests it showed she had cancer. I could not understand how she was absolutely fine three days before! She was running, playing, and jumping as she always did. There were no symptoms that she was even sick. We are devastated! I clearly remember the day I picked up Kimber from your house. She was absolutely beautiful, playing with her siblings in such a warm and loving environment. Hannah and Jake were great-looking parents with such a gentle demeanor that I knew immediately Kimber would grow up to be just like them.*

*Our children were so excited to meet her. We have all loved her since the day we brought her home. Our family loves being on the water and Kimber fit in perfectly. She went fishing with us in the boat, rode the jet-ski, and even rode the tube with our children. She enjoyed being with us as much as we loved being with her.*

*Kimber's favorite pastime was hunting minnows on the shoreline at our place in Mathews, Virginia. She would pounce on the minnows with her front paws and stick her head completely under the water, fishing for them. She would do this for hours. She also loved playing with her friend, Heidi. Heidi is our walker-beagle mix. Our daughter also has a cat, and Kimber was very gentle with her.*

*We asked our children what they will remember most about Kimber. Our daughter, Gracie, who is eleven, said she will remember all the days they played together in the yard or on the beach, swimming. Our trips to the Outer Banks and Mathews will never be the same. Our son, Riggs, who is thirteen, said he will miss her playfulness and great demeanor. She was such a good friend and obedient dog.*

*We enjoyed every minute of our six very short years with her. Our hearts ache knowing that she is no longer with us. Attached are a few pictures of our baby! I wish you the best on your book and look forward to reading it.*

> *Sincerely,*
> *Anita*

I was absolutely devastated to hear about Kimber. It was so sudden. My hope when I originally talked with Anita was to be able to tell a wonderful story about how happy their family was and how Kimber added joy to their lives. She did add much joy and happiness, but it did not last as long as it should have—the same as Dixie. I am so sad that they had to go through the same grief we have gone through in losing Dixie, and I hope this book will be a treasure to them, as it is to me; a way to remember how special they were.

## CHELSEA

Puppy number three was a black female with a large, triangular white mark on her chest. My best friend, Bev, wanted this pup as a Christmas surprise for her parents, Jim and Marie. We were so excited that they would have one of our pups. They are like family to us, so we would be able to see the pup often. We delivered the pup to our friends the day after Christmas. It was pouring rain as we went through Kilmarnock, heading for Wicomico Church, Virginia, which is on the Chesapeake Bay (a perfect place for a Labrador retriever), when, of course, the baby got carsick. All the pups were sensitive to travel—usually caused by being nervous about going to the vet. We found a church parking lot and pulled over to get her out of the car for a break and to clean up. We tied a red Christmas bow around her neck and snuck in the back door with the help of my friend, Bev, to try to keep this baby a surprise. It was so much fun watching the surprise and joy on their faces as we handed Chelsea over to them.

*Marie holding her new baby girl. Merry Christmas!*

*Baby Chelsea with Jim, Kendra and Susannah looking on*

*Chelsea loves her toys and usually wants you to toss them for her to retrieve*

*Chelsea after a groundhog!*

*Chelsea looking regal*

*Tobey and Dixie, hard to hold, excited to see Chelsea on the Chesapeake Bay*

*This plastic thingy tastes pretty good*

*Sleeping on her back just like she did as a puppy*

Jim and Marie named her Chelsea. She is truly a joy. She remembers us when we visit and gets so excited that she presses up against us to be loved on. The personality of each pup was different, but there were similarities between them as well. She likes to mouth your hands and arms like Dixie, and carries her toys around to get attention and tease you like Junior. She is a beauty, with light brown eyes and the sweetest disposition. What a blessing for Marie: Chelsea is her guardian and friend, and she walks with Jim to the mailbox every day. He has done a great job training her (he used to have hunting Labs), and she is so obedient, staying right by his side. She also likes to hunt, making her a great groundhog eliminator. She loves the water, just like her siblings, and enjoyed swimming in the creek that feeds into the Chesapeake Bay, until she found out about stinging nettles!

Marie wrote the following letter to us about Chelsea:

*After Rex died (the last of a long line of Labs), we decided we would not have another dog—it's just too hard to lose one. Then people who know better showed up at Christmas with a squirmy, happy black puppy with a big red bow around her neck (Thanks, friends!). She immediately captured our hearts. At bedtime, we planned that she would sleep in the bathtub, but she let us know that was not going to be. So she slept between us in our bed.*

*Friends soon appeared with a crate, which she liked and settled into. Chelsea was so easy to train (or she trained us) and has been a joy. She loves chasing squirrels from the bird feeders, and chasing groundhogs in the field. We know of at least six she has dispatched.*

*She is our official greeter and everyone loves her. She stays close by the yard and expects and gets her long walk each afternoon. She sleeps by our bed and wakes us up around 7 a.m. and waits patiently for Jim to get dressed so they can walk up the*

*lane to get the newspaper. Chelsea is the love of our life. Thanks,*
*Gail and Randy.*

### CHLOE

Puppy number four was a black female with a medium-sized white stripe on her chest. A woman named Ruth wanted to adopt this pup for her son Ryan's Christmas present. Ryan picked her out of the group and already had a name for her: Chloe. I had an opportunity to talk to Ruth about a year after they took her home; she expressed how amazed she was that Chloe was so good and smart. Ryan adores her.

*Chloe and Ryan on Christmas Eve*

Ruth sent this letter about Chloe:

*Chloe is Ryan's best friend, playmate, and lifelong companion.*
*When Chloe was a puppy, Ryan would take her on long walks*
*in the wooded trails in our neighborhood, where he would let her*
*play and swim in the creek. He would spend hours playing with*

*her and training her to do all kinds of tricks. Chloe is the one that can still put a smile on Ryan's face, even after a long, hard day at school and work.*

*Some of my favorite memories of Ryan and Chloe are of them swimming in the pool together. Chloe can dive in a little more than half the distance of the pool, especially when she feels the need to rescue Ryan when he, his cousins, and friends are horsing around in the pool. She protects him at all costs. When they're watching a football game or TV show, Chloe will jump up and bark at animals on the TV screen. It is so funny.*

*She loves guests coming over to visit. She is well behaved and so sweet. She loves everyone, especially my dad.*

*To this day, Chloe waits up for Ryan to come home, sleeps in his room with him, and gives him unconditional love. You see, Chloe is not just another puppy; she is an answer to a prayer, a gift heaven-sent, just for Ryan!*

*"Chloe," an answer to a prayer:*

*My son Ryan and I have lived with my younger brother, George, since Ryan was seven years old. George took us into his new home because I wanted Ryan to have a positive male role model in his life after my divorce. George soon loved Ryan like a son and did everything with him. To this day, fourteen years later, Ryan is like a son to George and he loves him very much. George has attended every life-changing event in Ryan's life. I do not know what we would have done without him in our lives.*

*So the decision to get another puppy for Ryan meant that George would have to agree and give us his blessing. That was going to take a miracle, since Ryan's yellow Lab, Lucky, had just passed away, and we all knew what a huge responsibility a puppy can be.*

*George swore he would never have another dog in his house again. Little did we know that God had other plans.*

*We'd moved in with George when Ryan was just about to turn seven years old, and to help with the transition, we adopted a yellow Lab from the Hanover Humane Society and surprised Ryan on his seventh birthday with his new dog. Ryan named the puppy Lucky, and he grew attached to his dog and companion. But like all puppies, Lucky had a learning curve that involved leaving a trail of hairballs throughout the house that ended up all over your clothes, chewing up furniture, having accidents on all the carpets in the house, and digging holes in the flowerbeds. George's new house was no longer the same beautiful home that he had spent months decorating. It had been taken over by this puppy's many mischievous endeavors. After five wonderful years, Lucky was now trained and was a big part of our family and we loved him.*

*One summer day, unexpectedly, Lucky became sick with a rare blood disorder, and we lost him after weeks of trying everything medically possible to keep him alive. It was a very sad time for the entire family and especially hard on Ryan. It was that day that George swore that he would never allow another dog in his home.*

*Months had gone by. It was a cool fall day, Ryan was now twelve years old, and I asked him what he wanted for Christmas. Ryan replied, "All I want is a puppy, but I want to pick him out myself." Of all the things a twelve-year-old could ask for, this one was going to be a big challenge. I was going to have to get George's approval, which was not an easy task. About a week later, after a nice home-cooked dinner, Ryan asked his uncle (whom he called Tío George) if he could get a puppy for Christmas. That is the only thing he wanted, no other toys or gadgets, just a puppy. The reply from George went something like this: "Absolutely not. No, no, no." Needless to say, Ryan walked away upset and discouraged.*

*When Ryan was upset or wanted to discuss something with me, he would lie on my bed right before bedtime to talk. I was reading my Bible when Ryan plopped himself down on my bed. In a soft and disheartened voice, he said, "Mom, I really want a puppy for Christmas, but you heard Tio George, and when he makes up his mind, he means what he says, no more dogs."*

*I paused for a moment and said, "Ryan, do you believe God answers our prayers?"*

*"Yes," he replied, "but this is different, Tio George is not going to change his mind."*

*I said, "I tell you what, the only person who can change a person's heart and mind is God. So we are going to pray every day now until Christmas for Tio George to let you have a puppy."*

*That is exactly what we did. Night after night, we prayed together. Ryan's bedroom was close enough to George's bedroom that George could overhear us praying aloud: "Jesus, please change Tio George's heart and mind and let Ryan have a puppy for Christmas." George shouted out, "You can pray all you want, but I am not changing my mind. No puppy." Ryan looked discouraged. I said, "Ryan, don't under estimate the power of prayer. You've got to have faith." We continued to pray night after night.*

*It was a chilly day in November when we all, including our niece Brittany, went on a family outing to the mall. Next to the mall was a PetSmart, where there were dogs outside in cages, hoping to be adopted by loving families. I asked George if we could stop for a minute, just so Ryan could pet the dogs. He reluctantly agreed. After about thirty minutes of watching Ryan pet all kinds of dogs with a big smile on his face, out of the blue, George said to Ryan, "Which dog do you like?" Ryan replied, "I can't decide, I like both of these dogs." George said, "Why don't we adopt them both, that way they can play with each other."*

*My jaw dropped and Ryan just looked at me in awe. Two dogs! What just happened? One minute, we cannot convince George to let us have one puppy, and the next, all of a sudden, he wants to let Ryan have two puppies. All I could say was "Does God answer prayer in a big way, praise the Lord!"*

*Then I went numb at the reality that I would have to feed, bathe, and take care of two dogs. Even if they were Ryan's dogs, the reality (which every parent quickly realizes) was that I would be taking care of these dogs and it was going to cost me a fortune. I suggested that we have lunch and discuss this before proceeding. Everyone unanimously agreed. Over a warm lunch, we laughed and we praised and thanked God. We prayed, "Thank you, Lord, for changing Tio George's heart and mind and letting Ryan have a dog. Please guide us to the puppy you want for Ryan." After that prayer, we decided that two dogs would be a little too much and thanked George for agreeing to let Ryan have a puppy and decided that we would let God help lead us in search for the right puppy.*

*Two weeks later, I saw an ad in the local paper for Lab puppies, and I arranged for Ryan and me to visit. I will never forget that day as long as I live. After our long drive, we finally arrived at the Canadas' home, where there were puppies everywhere—some playing, some sleeping, and some nestled next to their mom. We were both in awe at the sight. Ryan had originally wanted a male puppy, but when he picked up the last available male puppy and held it, it just wasn't the right one. Then he caught the eye of the sweetest, most playful female black Lab and he said, "Mom, can I change my mind and get the female pup instead? I really like her best." Luckily, she was still available. Randy and Gail sweetly agreed to hang on to our little puppy for us to pick her up on Christmas Eve, and diligently tagged her for Ryan. Ryan was so happy that day. I will never forget the big smile he had on his face. It was a reminder that God truly does hear our prayers. This puppy was an answer to our prayers, when we thought there was no hope.*

*Christmas Eve came and Ryan was up early that day, so excited and ready to pick up his new puppy, whom he had decided to name Chloe. Ryan is twenty-one years old now, and to this day, he will tell you that Chloe is the best Christmas gift he has ever received, and that he has never forgotten how blessed he is, how much his family loves him, and that Jesus loves him, hears his prayers, and answers them!*

*Football fan*

## JACKSON

Puppy number five was a small black male with a small white stripe on his chest. My long-longtime best friend, Pam (our adventures growing up together would fill another book), has a niece- and nephew-in-law who were interested in a pup for their three children: Hannah, the oldest; and twins Jake and Emily. I couldn't believe they had children named Hannah and Jake.

They named their pup Jackson. He was the smallest of the males, and he had Jake's head shape and was such a pretty boy. Pam helped raise him part of the time, taking him to the vet and so forth, since she is also the children's nanny and her niece's personal assistant.

This is the children's letter about Jackson, with Pam's assistance:

*Our puppy was a gift to us in 2007. We were ages seven and five that Christmas. He was the smallest of the litter, even though at ninety-nine pounds today, that is hard to remember. At first, Mom wasn't sure about having a dog, but he rode home in her lap and melted her heart. Of course, he had a little accident in her lap, too! We guess after having three kids, she was used to that.*

*We loved him from the moment he came home with us. We were asked what we wanted to name him and the three of us came up with the name "Goob." After that, we were just told his name would be Jackson.*

*Once he was named, we all started singing to him every day: "We got married in a fever, hotter than a pepper sprout; we've been talking about Jackson, ever since the fire went out!" We sang to him so much that even now, whenever anyone sings, he thinks it's all about him and gets excited!*

*We all went to obedience school with him. He is so smart that it did not take much effort to train him. He is such a well-mannered and respectful dog that everyone who comes to our house loves him.*

*Jackson loves to swim, chase squirrels up trees, and play with us in the yard. He loves to run with any "dog friend" that visits him. He is loyal and protective of us. Once, when running with our mom, he protected her against two large dogs that attacked her. He is a very important part of our family.*

*Jackson, we love you!!!*

*Hannah, Jake, and Emily*
*P.S. We also liked it that his mom was named Hannah and his dad was named Jake! LOL!*

*Jackson's first Christmas*

*Everyone's so grown up now!*

## Eli

Puppy number six was a larger black male with a small white stripe on his chest. A man named Marty answered our newspaper ad and adopted this pup for a friend of his, but then decided to keep him for himself. He named him Eli.

Marty wrote the following about Eli:

*I will tell you this: Eli is a big giant of a dog with a personality that is loving, protective, and caring. When Eli first came to us, it took him at least two weeks to accept us. He was withdrawn and leery of us. After a time, he started coming out of his crate, which remained open. But it seemed like that was his comfort zone, where he felt safe. As you will see in some of the pictures, he always had company in his crate. The pictures of Eli and my grandson, Brian, in the crate show you the bond they had between them. Brian used to ride him, and so Eli would walk up beside him, waiting for him to get on. It was a mutual thing that they enjoyed together. No one could do anything to harm Brian without going through Eli.*

*Eli also loves all the UPS drivers that come to the house. Being that I am the chief of the fire department, products are always being shipped to the residence and the UPS drivers always give him several dog biscuits. Because of his size, Eli is on a diet program. Right now, I think he's down to ninety-six pounds. At one time, he had tipped the scale at 105. He stays by my wife's and my side in the living room until someone starts turning off the lights to retire to bed. Then he's already stretched out beside the bed—he knows what time it is.*

*I've had many dogs, all of whom I loved; but I would have to say that Eli is as close to a person as any dog I've ever met. From his puppy years to his adult life, we pretty much came through it with him not getting hurt. On one occasion, he wandered off and got hit by a vehicle on US-522, but he just got a few bumps and bruises, no broken bones. That taught him that home-base is a safe place.*

*I'd also like to add that the picture of Eli and Brian means a lot to us, for we lost our grandson last year on January 12, and we miss him deeply.*

*Probably the funniest thing Eli does is that he will lie on his back to sleep. He also rubs his nose with both paws like a cat and holds his ball in both paws and plays with it. The only thing he needs is a pair of thumbs, and I guess he would be sitting at the dinner table. Let me close by saying that we really appreciate the fact that you let us have Eli, who is a wonderful companion. It just shows what kind of parents he had.*

*P.S. When we picked up Eli and saw his father, I wondered then if he would be as big a dog. Well, he made it! Thank you again. Martin.*

*Eli in the crate with Brian*

## Junior

Puppy number seven was a bigger, black male with a large white mark on his chest. He had big feet and looked just like his daddy, so we named him Junior.

*Jake watching over Junior*

*What's up?*

A young friend who used to dog-sit for us absolutely adored Jake and had always wanted a Jake puppy. She found out from our hairdresser that we had puppies and contacted us. We had almost decided to keep Junior, along with Dixie and Tobey, but our young friend assured us she would take good care of him and keep him safe. She couldn't pick him up until the end of January, which was fine with us. It meant he could stay home a bit longer. Being a young woman who was financially challenged, our friend was working two jobs and was not home much. She ended up keeping Junior in a horse stall during the day with her other dog, a Jack Russell. The Jack Russell picked on him relentlessly. Junior still has white flecks of hair on his head from bite scars. The horse stall may have also caused him to be deathly afraid of horse flies.

One winter day a year later, we got a call from our friend; she wanted to meet up for a play day with Junior. We were so excited to have a chance to see him. A date was set, but two days prior, we got another call. Junior had gotten away from her and had run off with a neighbor's dog. She didn't find him until the next day. He had been hit by a truck or car and almost died. I was devastated and wished we had kept him. Fortunately, his owner worked for an emergency veterinary clinic part-time and rushed him there. It took several months for him to regain his mobility and elimination functions. We sent her money to help with the cost of his therapy. She was able to get him chiropractic and acupuncture sessions and was really dedicated to making him better. He has a broken pelvis and nerve damage to his rectum, meaning he has trouble controlling his bowels to this day. He does really well now, running with everyone else in the field or on the trail, or swimming in the river (it took him a few tries to learn how to swim). He does have a limp, and runs a bit like he's dancing the Watusi, with his back legs swinging out to each side.

Even after all that, Junior still isn't car-smart. We have to be careful driving up to the house, because we're afraid he won't get out of the way. He has this habit of meeting you with a big grin as you get out of the car, a huge stick in his mouth—his gift to you for coming home. I'm always afraid he'll poke one of the other dogs in the eye with that stick. He is such a lover and just wants attention. When we're in the house, he'll bring one of his stuffed toys to you. He won't actually give it to you; he just wants you to pay attention and pet him. Once you've petted him, he'll take his toy and climb up on the sofa, satisfied. He'll end up on his back, sound asleep.

I guess you're wondering how he ended up back with us. Our young friend was planning a trip to Canada to work with horses. We had told all the puppies' owners that if they ever needed someone to puppy-sit, they could bring them to our house for free. We did that with Jackson a couple of times as well. He was trained to comply with the invisible fence, and we had a collar for him, which was really convenient. One day, though, upon returning home from work after a severe thunderstorm, we couldn't find Jackson anywhere. We freaked! The storm had frightened him so badly that he'd run through the fence. We searched for him, found him, and brought him back to safety. He must have gotten that from Hannah. She is frightened by thunder and lightning, too. She doesn't bolt, though; she just hides under your leg (whether you are standing or not).

So Junior came back to us temporarily while his owner traveled. This was in April. Junior was eighteen months old. She planned to pick him up in August or September, depending on her work. She called shortly after she left to ask how he was, but come August, we didn't hear from her. So, we called her in September, only to find out that she hadn't ended up in Canada at all: she was in Georgia; the job didn't work out. Where did that leave Junior? Since she didn't have a permanent job or a place to live, we decided we'd keep Junior until things changed in her life. As you have probably figured out, we still have Junior.

It was a little bit of a trial introducing him back into the group. It was like he was the stepchild, having been left out of the learning experiences Dixie and Tobey had. He wasn't confident in playing with them (probably because of the encounters with the Jack Russell). At first, Tobey would get jealous and start fights with Junior. This just terrified us, and we struggled to find a solution to these conflicts. Tobey is generally very sensitive to corrective words—unless he's in the middle of a fight. Then you have to get across to him that what he did was wrong without hurting his feelings. We caught him in the act, which is the best time to correct bad behavior; but the altercations happened twice more after that. We don't know what sparked the fights, but Junior always bore the brunt of it. The last time, most recently, I fed Junior first, then turned them outside as usual. We heard a scrap and ran outside to break it up. Junior came in limping, with the hair on his back standing up. Nobody ever gets hurt really bad—just a few bites and hurt legs—but it's disturbing. So now, we make sure Tobey always eats first. It's the animal kingdom: there's a pecking order. With horses, it's the same thing. We feed the alpha gelding first so that he feels special and all the others know he's the boss. This helps him with his status in the herd and he doesn't have to demonstrate his dominance to the others.

Junior is at the bottom of the pecking order because he wasn't raised with the others. He'll play with Dixie, but not so much with Tobey, and he will roughhouse with Hannah.

Junior fits in fine now. He loves to sleep on the sofa or bed and loves to go to the river. He learned how to swim from Dixie. He's a little slow about getting in the truck—everybody else hops in anxious for an adventure, but he's just not in a hurry about much of anything except meals. He's our turtle dog: he can sniff out a turtle within a half mile and carry it, no matter how far, back to the truck. There he gets a treat to replace the turtle, which is released to be caught again. He also surprises me by finding tennis balls that have been lost for months (sometimes he's the one that loses them—but only if he gets distracted by turtle scent!).

*Junior playing with Dixie in the river*

*Junior learned to swim by watching Dixie at the river.*

*Junior loves his toys.*

## DIXIE

Puppy number eight was a yellow female with a small white diamond on her forehead, black footpads, a black nose, and a black "z" on her hind leg.

We chose this pup for ourselves because of her personality, sweet disposition, and antics, and we named her Dixie.

*My sweet baby girl*

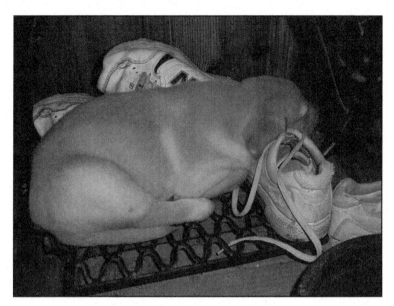

*Dixie loved shoes—either to sleep on or chew on!*

*Our 2007 Christmas card—too many to count or hold onto!*

*Dixie loved tennis balls—she'd toss them up in the air with her front paws and play with them. Who needs a human to toss them for her?*

*Tobey and Dixie in their favorite place—which meant we had to buy another sofa for us.*

*Dixie and Jake lounging in the backyard*

*Caught in the act*

*Dixie and Tobey in a well-dug-up backyard with Hannah watching over them*

*She loved to relax on the sofa.*

Dixie had the cutest personality. She would sometimes just stare at us like she was studying us. Her hind legs were slightly bowed, making her wiggle when she ran, but that didn't slow her down any. She was very quick to catch Tobey in their chase games. Tobey and Dixie, as well as Hannah, would accompany us to the basement when we worked out. They loved to wrestle on the carpeted floor and play tug-of-war with an old rag. She loved getting in the dog truck for adventures in the fields or on the trails. The stuffed squeaky toys I would bring home were her favorite things. Her main interest was in tearing them apart to get that squeaker. I would toss stuffed monkeys in the field for the dogs to retrieve, but Dixie would run with her monkey and want me to chase her—she loved to play those games.

Dixie would experience some anxiety whenever we were gone for a day or two, and, upon returning, we would find a dog bed demolished on the porch, stuffing everywhere. She wanted us to know that we were missed. There was not a mean bone in her body; she never growled at the others over anything. I'm not saying she didn't enjoy getting in on chasing a squirrel, skunk, or other furry animal.

Dixie was such a lover, and always wanted to cuddle. Sitting on the sofa, she would put her head in your lap or on your shoulder just to love on you and have you love on her. She had a tendency to lick your face and ears as well. She loved body lotion, too, and would come into the bathroom after my shower and lick most of the lotion off my legs. She also liked to put her head in the shower, because she loved the water. On our river outings, her joy was just swimming up and down the river, pushing a tennis ball, and at times becoming distracted and losing the ball to the current. Her front paws she used like hands, pawing my leg for a treat or attention, pawing the doors to let us know she wanted to come into the house, and actually throwing a ball up in the air with them for a game of catch with herself.

## Tawny

Puppy number nine was a yellow female whose coat was caramel in color. I nicknamed her "Reba" after the wildfire redhead Reba McEntire. When she went to her new home, she was renamed Tawny.

Reba got into mischief when she was living with us.

One Sunday morning, we left the puppies out in the yard because we weren't going to be gone long. We had just gotten back from feeding the horses, came in the front door of the house before going out back to check on everyone, and heard a yelp. I ran out back to find Reba at the bottom of the basement steps. She had gotten over the barricade, walked onto the tarp, and fallen through to the bottom step of the basement. We could tell she was hurt, her front leg in particular. It being a Sunday (go figure), I rushed her to the emergency clinic. They X-rayed her leg, and sure enough, it was broken: a clean fracture, but still broken. They put a cast on it and instructed me to keep her quiet. Then we had to figure out how to keep her off the leg and not let the other pups jump on her.

The solution was a child's playpen that we borrowed from Curtis, a good friend of ours, and whose family has been my family's friends and neighbors for as long as memory serves. Reba was supposed to be his pup; he had chosen her as a surprise Christmas present for his wife and children. When I called him to let him know what had happened, I told him we would keep her and he could take the other available female pup— that would be Dixie. He was adamant about his selection and wanted to keep Reba, broken leg and all. Things always turn out for the best. We delivered her on Christmas morning, with red and green bandages wrapped around her cast.

*This cast is a bit awkward.*

*I can still play ball!*

Once she'd healed, Curtis would bring her over to visit and play with Dixie and Tobey, and it amazed us that there was no indication her leg had ever been broken. It was as good as new. She just loved to play with our pups and Curtis would say she never acted as excited as she did when she saw me. I truly think they remember who their "real" momma is.

*Christmas morning: Curtis, Anita, Meghan, and Jared with Santa's Tawny!*

Curtis and his family wrote the following about Tawny:

*We got Tawny for Christmas 2007, but before we got her from Gail and Randy, she fell down the basement steps and broke her front leg. Trying to housetrain a puppy that can't get her cast wet was not very easy, especially in the winter weather. She is an eighty-pound female with just a single black speck on her hind leg. She loves all people, no matter color, gender, or age, and she never barks when a new person comes over. She doesn't have a mean bone in her body toward humans, but she either hates cats or loves to chase them. Cats, squirrels, groundhogs, and snakes— they are all the same to her. She will eat absolutely anything that is fed to her, whether it's nutritious, junk food, dog food, or human food. Her favorite things to do with our daughter, Meghan, are greeting her when she pulls into the driveway and sitting next to her while she does homework at the kitchen table. With our son, Jared, she enjoys playing fetch and following him up and down the driveway as he runs. We love Tawny, and there is no doubt that she loves us. She is very gentle, loving, loyal, and smart. She loves rides in the truck, and she loves visiting my parents, mostly to chase cats and play in the creek. With all of her pros and cons, her ups and downs, we may have other dogs, but we will never have another Tawny.*

*Curtis and Anita with Tawny*

*They are all grown up!*

*Do you have a treat for me?*

## Bucky

Puppy number ten was a light-yellow male, large in size, with a black nose and black toe pads. He looked just like our Tobey. Eddie also saw our newspaper ad and wanted to adopt this pup for a Christmas gift for his grandson Jake. The pup was named "Bucky."

We talked to Jake's granddad on the phone, and he said that Bucky is the most amazing dog. He just loves the kids and is so laid-back.

Jake and Seth's mother, Susie, wrote the following letter about Bucky:

*Jake and Seth got Bucky for Christmas in 2007. Jake was five and Seth was two. Bucky was absolutely adorable and still is. He brought joy to our family immediately. I really think we got the best Lab puppy and dog anybody could have asked for. He was not a very rowdy puppy; he didn't chew up stuff like puppies usually do. We didn't have to spend a lot of time on training; he just caught on very quickly. He always wanted and still wants to please—and he does. We can count on Bucky to put a smile on our faces. He actually smiles at us when we come home, and that will just melt your heart.*

*He has the best temperament. Bucky loves everybody, and everybody who comes in contact with him loves him also. He loves to go swimming in the river with the boys, and they also love it when he swims with them. He is just 120 pounds of pure sweetness. Seth says, "He is awesome, cute, and my favorite dog in the world." He sleeps in between the boys. That can be a little tight—he is a big boy.*

*Bucky loves skunks and can sometimes smell awful. I think one week he got sprayed every night. Jake says he is "the greatest dog in the whole world! He is a great hunting dog and the best pillow ever." I really don't know what we will ever do without him. He truly is the best.*

    *Thanks so much,*

    *Susie*

*Looks comfortable! The boys think he's a pillow.*

*Bucky's recliner!*

*Everyone's still sleeping on their backs!*

*Getting a little big for that recliner! Switched places.*

*Bucky with his best snow buds. Looks a bit cold!*

*Virginia fans*

*He's so handsome!*

## Gage

Puppy number eleven was a caramel-colored male. A woman named Angel adopted him as a Christmas present for her children, Brittany and Steven. There were advertisements on TV for Charmin toilet paper featuring the cutest yellow Lab puppy rolling toilet paper all over the house. Angel's children wanted the little Charmin pup, as seen on those commercials. They named him Gage.

Unfortunately, after several attempts to contact the family, I never received a story or photos and am very disappointed not to be able to share his story.

## Tobey

Puppy number twelve is my Tobey. He's a chunky yellow male, light-colored, with a black nose and toe pads. He was the largest of the yellow males and now weighs in between 110 and 120 pounds, and is long like his daddy, Jake. He is the main man here; everyone follows his lead. He is the most energetic and adventurous, always looking for something to chase or hunt. When we arrive home from a workday, he is the first one at the car door to greet us. Usually, immediately after our greeting, he runs to the dog truck, jumping up and down enthusiastically, asking for his field trip. He loves to sit on the sofa next to me, putting his head on my shoulder or just wanting to be close. He will follow me from room to room if I am working at home, just to lie down beside my chair. His daddy, Jake, used to do the same thing; even in the kitchen while I would be fixing their meals, I would have to step over him to work at the kitchen counter.

Tobey will always get in the bed at night and lay his head on my stomach to sleep. He rarely spends all night there, because he gets hot and goes to sleep in the dog bed on the floor; but he always returns to bed before we get up in the morning. If Randy is a little late getting out of bed, Tobey will climb in bed to help him get up. Sometimes, because of his size, he accidentally ends up pinning Randy under the covers.

Tobey is my guardian: he worries over me if I start coughing at night. He climbs in the bed, if he is not already there, and stands up, looking over my face until I stop. Anyone who drives up our long driveway is greeted with Tobey barking, hair standing on end, like he is truly the watchdog. But as soon as they get out of their vehicle, he is over that and ready to receive any rubs our visitors would like to give.

Tobey and Dixie were very close. When Dixie was sick, Tobey would lie down next to her, lick her ears, and love on her, but he would never lick her sutures. It was as if he knew he shouldn't do that. After Dixie was gone, Tobey would still search for her. He seemed so lost. It seems that he has become more attached to me, not straying too far from me when I am home. You can tell he really misses his sister and playmate.

*My sweet boy, Tobey, watching me fix his dinner.*

*Tobey looking all innocent*

*Tobey with his hair on fire!*

*Tobey learning how to build a fire*

*Enjoying that fire on a winter's day*

*Tobey thought his mom was comfortable.*

*Jake with Tobey and Dixie, sharing one of their beds*

*Hence the nickname Tobaroo! He can hop straight up like a kangaroo when excited, just like his daddy, Jake!*

# 7

## Mitzie's Story

My kinship with animals, particularly dogs, started with Mitzie. She was a purebred collie that was the same age I was, which meant, for a long time, I didn't know life without her. She was my best friend and so smart. She knew exactly what I was saying when I talked to her. Momma raised collies, and Mitzie was the best puppy maker. She would have her puppies on a bed momma made for her in the clay basement under the kitchen. When she wanted to feed her pups, she would come to the barn or wherever we were and lead us back to the basement to move her pups so she could lie down with them without hurting them.

When I was six years old, my daddy got a pony and cart for me. Without hesitation, Mitzie would hop up in the cart to go for a ride with me. I played with her and the other animals on the farm instead of children my own age. Granted, the other children weren't just next door—the closest neighbor was at least a mile away—but I think I preferred animals over people. Mitzie always wanted to play the games I wanted to play, never any arguments.

She was very protective of us as well. My cousin, who spent part of every summer with us, would try to pick on me, but Mitzie would be by my side, growling with teeth bared, protecting me. My momma revealed to me that when she was a pup, a man had thrown a brick at her, and she'd never forgotten it. No man could get out of his vehicle at our house safely, because she would be barricading the perimeter. After reading puppy care and training

86

manuals, I learned that pups remember everything that happens to them from the time they open their eyes at three weeks of age.

When Mitzie and I were both thirteen, Momma asked me to go with her to take Mitzie to the vet. She had tumors in her mouth and was losing teeth, which was causing her trouble eating. The tumors had actually developed on her hips as well. I didn't go into the clinic with them, and Momma came out without her. I don't believe I'd known she wouldn't be coming home with us. Momma explained that she was sick and wouldn't get any better. For her sake, it was better to let her sleep, so she wouldn't suffer through a painful illness.

I had a hard time understanding that they couldn't cure her. I have a personality that makes me want to fix things. I remember sobbing all the way home and then some. I truly don't remember when my grieving stopped. Everything in my childhood memory included Mitzie. I couldn't help but feel angry with my mother for not trying to save her somehow. When you are young, it's hard to understand death.

I've always felt I should have gone into veterinary medicine. I love science and was a biology major in college, but I just didn't have the patience to stay in school long enough to earn a degree. I still love to doctor our horses and other animals when necessary, but I get so attached to my "patients," I don't know if I could administer "sleep" if I were to become a real veterinarian.

# 8

## Muffin's Story

When the puppies were little, we still had Muffin. We had to watch her around the pups, because she would nip at them and hurt their feelings. She had gotten very old and didn't tolerate those playful little things jumping around her or being curious about her.

Muffin's name was short for Ragamuffin. She was a beagle who had been used for hunting before she came to us. Hunters have a bad reputation for dropping their hunting dogs off on the side of the road if they aren't producing or living up to expectation. And that's the sad reality that led Muffin to us.

I was doing my daily run on Petersburg Road when I noticed a pair of beagles running away, frightened at the sight of me. I figured they were hunting dogs, possibly lost, but they didn't seem interested in being recovered and were spooked by my presence. I had seen them on the road occasionally for a couple of months. One day I found one of the beagles in the ditch, killed by a car, but I didn't see the other one. A few days later, I found the other beagle lying in the ditch, curled up in a fetal position, waiting to die of starvation. I ran home, got the car and a blanket, and rushed back to rescue her from the ditch.

She was barely alive. She opened her mouth, but I couldn't tell whether she was trying to bite me or talk. She was so frail, nothing but skin covering bone. I gave her water and fed her canned dog food by hand. She couldn't eat much at a time. I didn't want to traumatize her with a vet visit until she had gained some strength.

After about seven days, I took her to Bill. He determined that she was three years old and had given birth to puppies at one point. She had been hit by a car and had nerve damage in her front shoulder. She would stick her leg straight out in front of her or sometimes drag it, but she still managed to get around pretty well. We had her vaccinated and on the road to recovery.

Muffin didn't want anything to do with our other dogs. She'd growl and snap at them, leading us to suspect she'd been beaten up by other dogs over food. Randy made her a nice house behind the back shed and we'd take her food and check on her. She didn't run off; I guess she figured she had a good thing. In time—not long at all actually—she decided she would rather be closer to the house. She would come closer and closer until she ended up on the back stoop. She fell in love with our Lab, Sadie, and stayed close to her, as if for protection. She wasn't housebroken, so that was a challenge. She did finally get the hang of it. If she wanted to stay in the house, she'd better do her business outside; if she had an accident, out she went!

She would also gobble her food as fast as possible. Afterward, we'd let her out of the house and watch her go into the woods and throw it up. She would then bury it. We learned that dogs who have been starved learn to save their food by upchucking and burying it. They will go back later to dig it up for another meal. It's a survival instinct. It took two or three years for her to feel like she didn't have to do that any longer—the meals would always be there for her.

She was really sweet, and what a talker! Beagles have a kind of howling-yodel-type bark. She usually did this when she saw us coming home or wanted to come inside with us, or was requesting dinner. She really responded to affection—absolutely loved it. I don't think she'd ever had any before.

Over time, Muffin became really frail, lost weight, and couldn't eat regular dog food. She started losing teeth, and it was hard for her to chew hard food. The older she became, the more she reverted back to not controlling her bowels or bladder as well. When she started peeing in the house, we made her stay on a bed on the porch. Then we got her a doghouse on the porch for cooler weather, and put a heating blanket in it for her in the winter. When the porch got really nasty from her not being able to get off of it to do her business, we took her house to the outdoor kennel and set it up with blankets and an extension cord for her electric blanket. At this point, I was feeding her chicken soup and she was having a hard time eating enough of that to keep any weight on. We knew it was time. We didn't feel so bad about having her sleep, because she'd had a long, happy life—a much better life with us than she would have had with her previous owners. She was sixteen years old.

## 9

## *Field Trips*

With Muffin gone and ten of the pups adopted, we were left with Tobey and Dixie, in addition to Hannah and Jake. Hannah and the pups slept in the bed with us. As the pups grew, the sleeping space dwindled. A king-size bed was required! Then our sitting space in the living room got smaller, requiring another sofa. The puppies were growing to be the size of people, and liked to sit next to us, watching TV.

The puppies seemed to get carsick every time they rode in the van. So we decided to take them on some short, fun trips to try to acclimate them to travel. We started taking them up to the barn with us in the "dog truck" twice a day to feed the horses. After feeding the horses, we'd take them to play ball in the field. These fun trips worked; they stopped getting carsick and now loved to go for a ride.

Jake loved to go along, too. He didn't chase the ball that much because of his back, but he liked to roll and scratch his back in the grass and explore new smells. We had to help him into the van, but he could get out without too much trouble.

Hannah would excitedly jump up and down to chase a ball. She would keep after us to throw it the whole time we were out in the field. She would actually bring us the ball and bounce it in front of us, signifying that she wanted us to throw it for her. Tobey and Dixie loved to chase a ball, too. It had to be a squeaky one for Dixie, though. She thought it was great fun to get it and run away with it squeaking the whole time, hoping you'd chase her. Tobey wouldn't bring it back, either; he would just lose interest and drop it.

One day while shopping at the dollar store, I found some stuffed monkeys with squeakers in them that sounded like monkey talk and decided to buy four of them. The puppies loved them! They were so surprised by the talking monkeys. They would cock their heads in confusion. The stuffed monkeys didn't have a long life: there were monkey parts all over the van. That would be Dixie's doing. Plus, they were great for tug-of-war between Dixie and Tobey. The stuffed ducks we had were good too, emitting a quack instead of a squeak. It was so much fun to see the puppies' reactions to the different sounds. In retrospect, those toy choices may not have been such a good idea. I wonder if they made the pups want to attack small furry animals (like skunks!).

When Dixie reached six months of age, we decided to have her spayed. We also knew that we only wanted Hannah to have

*Picnic trip: Dixie, Hannah, and Tobey,*
*with Jake in the shade next to the dog truck*

one litter of pups—she'd already had enough for two! Her little belly was so stretched out of shape, we didn't think she'd ever get her girlish figure back. So the girls had their operation on the same day so they could recuperate together.

It's hard to keep a puppy relaxed and quiet. It's easier if there are two confined rather than one. We barricaded them on the porch with their dog beds and a bucket of water during the day, and, of course, they were in the house as soon as we got home. It didn't take them long to be back to chasing balls like before.

On hot summer days, we'd take everybody, including Jake, to our good friend Gary's farm, which backs up to the Appomattox River. The area next to the river is probably 2.5 miles from the main road, so we didn't have to worry about the pups getting into trouble. They had such a nice place to enjoy the river: a sandy beach and steps down the steep, fifteen-foot bank to the river for human guests. The pups and Hannah didn't need the steps; they would just bound off down the bank to the water for a refreshing dip, or to fetch an elusive ball.

*On the riverbank*

*Tobey and Junior enjoying a swim*

*All four enjoying the cool river's current*

Jake could get down the bank via the steps pretty well with some assistance, but we'd have to help him get back up the bank when we headed home. He loved to just lounge in the water at the edge of the river.

The pups had played in streams, before but never in deeper water. Their first experience with the river was quite a bit different. Hannah already knew how to swim, and Dixie jumped in and followed after her mother, proving herself a natural swimmer. Tobey, on the other hand, jumped up and down in the water, slapping with his front feet, fighting the water. He finally got the hang of it and enjoyed getting into the deep water, swimming over to explore the other side of the riverbank.

If we went during the week, it was usually deserted, giving us our own private beach. The dogs loved to jump into the river after balls, or just to cool off. Hannah was always asking us to throw the ball—then she'd take it and swim with it. Dixie would swim up by her side, trying to steal it, and they would end up swimming up and down the river, carrying the ball in their mouths, only to lose interest or get distracted, releasing many balls that got away downstream. Tobey and Dixie would chase each other up the bank to go explore the nearby trees. Next thing you knew, Dixie would be chasing Tobey down the bank and into the water, where she usually caught him. Both Dixie and Tobey would bring those tennis balls onshore and toss them up in the air, grab them with both front paws and bury them in the sand, dig them up, toss them, and bury them again. It was so much fun to watch, but you had to keep an eye on the ball or you'd lose it in the sand. They would play with the balls in the snow in the same way.

One summer afternoon after a heavy rain, the river was high and the current was stronger than usual. Dixie, our water dog, went swimming away, ending up a little too far downstream. We called her to come back, but it was like she was in one of those exercise pools: she kept swimming as hard as she could without getting anywhere! Randy had to swim in after her and help her back to shore. She was a tired pup that night.

The pups enjoyed their first snow—what an adventure! They loved running in it and burying their noses in it, trying to smell it or whatever was under it. We lost so many tennis balls in the field under the snow! It was fun finding them when the snow melted.

*Hey, Mom, is there a ball under there?*

*Hey, what's this white stuff? Does it smell?*

*It's fun running in this cool stuff!*

*Last Christmas photo with Jake*

# 10

## Jake's Challenge

That spring, Jake still enjoyed getting in the dog truck and playing in the fields behind the barn. He'd long needed help getting into the truck, but now he needed a little help getting out of it as well. One day I noticed him favoring his front leg. I didn't know whether, in getting in and out of the truck, he had pulled or strained it, or whether, because sometimes I had to wrap my arms under his chest and lift him out, I had accidentally pulled on him and hurt him. It got worse, not better, and he was already on pain medication and anti-inflammatories for his back.

We went back to see Dr. Bill. An X-ray was taken. It showed a bone cancer tumor in the leg.

I couldn't believe what I was hearing. I was devastated! Bone cancer, we found out, is quite painful. More pain medication was prescribed, as well as a pain patch we could put directly over the tumor spot. At his age, with his current health issues, there was nothing that could be done to extend his life or improve his quality of life. They said the cancer would eventually go to his lungs or other parts of his body. We could do nothing but try to make him comfortable, and cry, because it was inevitable that we would lose him.

I am a very light sleeper. I guess it's the mothering instinct to listen for your children. I'd get up many times during the night—if Jake's medication was to be taken every four hours, he got it every four hours.

He made it through the second Christmas with the pups feeling pretty good. Then, in March, he started having seizures. I was terrified. I called Bill and he told me what to do over the phone. He thought it might be an insulin imbalance; we needed to feed him before his shot, instead of after as we'd been doing for several years.

The seizures caused Jake's muscles to spasm and he would lose consciousness for a few minutes, which would upset Hannah and the pups, so we needed to get him outside. He was still a very big dog at 125 pounds, and it was hard to carry him. We ended up rolling him onto a blanket and pulling the blanket out with him lying on it. After being outside for a few minutes, he would regain his composure and be back to normal.

One morning in early April, he had another seizure. This time he lost control of his bladder, peeing all over the kitchen floor. I was trying to help him, bawling uncontrollably at the same time. He regained awareness and looked startled, as though wondering what had just happened. We got him outside on a blanket next to the water bucket. He perked up. He was lying down but had his head up, watching us and whatever was going on around him. The pups must have sensed something was wrong, because they left him alone. He seemed like he'd recovered and would be okay that day, so I went on to my work appointments. Randy would be home with him.

Randy called me a couple of hours later; Jake wasn't doing well. He just didn't look right and seemed disoriented. Randy felt that Jake needed to see Dr. Bill. Our friend, Gary, rushed over to help Randy pick Jake up and put him in the truck for that trip to Bill's.

I was on an appointment miles away, on the other side of Mechanicsville near Tappahannock, when the clinic called me on my cell. It seemed the tumors had spread throughout Jake's body and brain. They asked if I wanted to see him to say goodbye before they let him sleep. I was so grief-stricken, all I could do was wail. I couldn't talk or stop crying. And I couldn't bear the thought of him being put to sleep before my eyes. It was really hard on Randy. That was April 1, 2009.

We requested that Jake have a private cremation and be returned to us. His ashes are in an urn sitting on our living room pie safe, with his dog tags and a statue of a black Lab beside them.

That same afternoon, our friend Tommy delivered a load of gravel we had ordered several days before for our driveway. It was late afternoon, the time we usually feed the horses. Randy had already gone out to help Linda, a friend and boarder, with feeding, since I couldn't talk to people without breaking down. Meanwhile, I took Hannah, Dixie, and Tobey for their afternoon run. Tobey is really persuasive about getting that run in.

Soon after we left, Tommy showed up with the gravel. The sides of the driveway at the creek must have washed away some, for the next thing we knew, the dump truck slid off the road, tipping on its side. Randy had been riding on the running boards of the truck, directing Tommy where to dump the gravel. This left Randy hanging onto the sides of the truck for dear life! If it hadn't been for a tree growing up beside the drive at the creek's edge, that truck would have been lying on its side in the creek. We named that tree "Tommy's Tree," because it saved him from injury or worse.

The dilemma now was how to get the gravel off the truck (because it weighed it down) and how to get the truck back up the steep hill. Along came the farmer musketeers: our friends Gary and Wayne, plus Tommy's boys and my cousin Sammy, to save the day. They had to shovel the gravel off the truck, and then figure out how to hook the dump truck to two tractors to pull it back up the hill. That took several hours. I guess sometimes God gives you diversions to allow you to escape some of your grief.

Because of all this, I couldn't drive the dog truck back home via the driveway. The pups and Hannah were so good. I parked the truck, took their shock collars off, and walked them home through the woods. Since we had the invisible fence for Jake, Hannah had learned from him and was sensitive to the fence line. She remembered getting zapped once going across it. We had to go over to the line, reach across it to take her collar off, and coax her back to the enclosed yard. Even with the collar off, she knew where the line was and had to be led through it.

Dixie was too smart; if she got close to the line and didn't hear the beep, she'd just follow her nose wherever it took her. We found her up at the new barn one afternoon having an adventure! This made us aware that the invisible fence was *not* working and needed immediate repair. We eventually got her a nine-volt battery collar like we had for Tobey and Jake; they all had that strong hunter instinct.

It was past dark when Randy got back to the house. I don't know if we ate dinner that night. All we could do was cry together. I'm not sure how long it took before we could talk to each other or to others about Jake without choking back tears. I still tear up over losing him.

# 11

## *Being Siblings*

The puppies were about eighteen months old when Jake passed. They were just full of themselves. We vowed to make sure they got plenty of exercise so they wouldn't get overweight like Jake and have health issues. Since we went to the barn twice a day to feed the horses, that was a good time to take them with us in the dog truck for an outing, such as a run in the fields or on the trails we'd recently cut through the back part of our property to give our boarders additional space to ride their steeds.

Dixie loved to act like a lioness stalking Tobey. She would crouch down in the tall grass, hiding from him. He'd pretend he didn't see her, and she would sneak slowly, getting into position to pounce. When the time was right, she'd charge. He knew she was going to get him. He would run back and forth and in circles, trying to outrun her, but she would always cut him off. I think he liked that she always caught him. These antics were so much fun to watch. They would also play hide-and-seek in the yard around the big oak tree, or wrestle on the floor together—just like children. I never broke it up; I knew they wouldn't hurt each other.

There was a time when I used to worry about the house being clean, and didn't like dogs licking my face. But with those babies, it didn't matter. I loved their licks, and the house was just not important. We did replace the living room and kitchen rugs after the other ten pups left; that was definitely necessary! Dixie thought we'd bought them just for her; they smelled so new that she immediately chewed a corner off each rug. She also loved to rest on the sofa, with me or without me, watching Randy and me over the back of the sofa as we fixed the dogs' dinner in the kitchen.

*TV time*

*My "Doodle" girl waiting for dinner*

Even when we came home from work, they would all run out to greet us: Tobey was usually first, wanting to be petted; Dixie would vie for position, grabbing my arm; and Junior would follow with a big stick as his gift. Hannah would hang back until everybody else was done.

Tobey's main goal was to get in the dog truck for an outing. He would greet me and then run to the truck, hopping up and down like a kangaroo—expressing his wish to go and play. They loved to get in the truck and go exploring; new smells were everywhere. I don't think it had anything to do with the bag of treats behind the driver's seat, which they got when they got back in the truck.

One afternoon in late spring, Dixie wouldn't stand on her hind leg. She held it up off the ground, as if it was painful to put any weight on it. I took her to see Dr. Bill. She had a ruptured ACL, just like people can get. I found out that this is more common in dogs, particularly large dogs, than I would have thought. Dixie was a big baby and she seemed a little bow-legged in the back. She probably ruptured it during one of those hide-and-seek games with Tobey.

We were supposed to keep her quiet for twenty-one days to give it time to heal on its own. Randy rigged a blockade on the front porch, with her bed and a bucket of water for the times we weren't home during the day. She was so good, but she couldn't restrain herself from getting excited when we got home. Do you know how hard it is to keep a two-year-old puppy quiet? But she did recover, and didn't have to have surgery. She recovered so well that a few months later, we noticed Tobey wouldn't raise his tail when we were running in the field. At first I thought he was upset about something and that his feelings were hurt; but then I realized he couldn't. Dixie must have damaged his tail by pulling it during one of their chases. It took almost two weeks before he could raise it again.

We tried to give them some variety in their outings. We took them to Millquarter Lake one hot summer afternoon (thanks to my niece belonging to the homeowner's association). There was really deep water there, and it was so much fun actually swimming with our pups. Other members of Millquarter would frequently walk their dogs by the lake, and I was a bit concerned about how Tobey would act around dogs he did not know, particularly since he had not been neutered. But all of our pups were always so good and well behaved.

We loved going to the river behind Gary's, and during the summer, we would go once or twice a week. Sometimes Gary's family and kids would be down there fishing, and our dogs loved swimming with them. The children would toss a ball for them to fetch out of the river. Hannah in particular never wanted to stop, but Tobey and Dixie would get bored and start exploring.

One Sunday afternoon, we piled the dogs into the dog truck for an hour-long ride to the river behind cousin Donna's farm for a picnic with Donna, her grandchildren, and Aunt Anne. Then we made a lengthy trip to visit our friends and Chelsea, on the Chesapeake Bay, where they could jump off the dock and into the creek. Our pups loved the water!

At certain times of the year, geese would flock and graze in the horse pasture. Since the horses are kept in the "fatty" paddock at night, I could drive the dog truck out on the field before we let the horses out. Opening the gate carefully so as not to spook the geese, we'd drive slowly, trying to get in close enough range for the dogs to think they might be able to catch one of these flying fowl. From inside the van, I would tell everyone to stay, then open the doors quietly and say, "Okay!" Tobey was out like a rocket, nearly catching those geese, and Dixie was right on his heels, with Junior and Hannah trailing behind, not so excited about the goose chase. I think Hannah would have preferred chasing a tennis ball. She's not that interested in flying things. Tobey and Junior would both look to the sky to chase flying birds—the girls, not so much. Goose droppings are not good for horses to be around, but after being chased a few times, the geese would decide to go elsewhere to feed, and our fun and games would end up being beneficial.

In the fall, the pear trees in the field behind the new barn were a favorite place for the dogs as well as the deer. All the dogs loved to eat those pears. I would pick up a bunch and throw them like balls. They would chase them and retrieve them, but they never brought them back to me! A lot of the time, I would just use them as treats, and wait until they got close to the dog truck before throwing them—then they would hop in the truck with their pears, munching away.

Dixie had a knack for finding something stinky to roll in. If I didn't see her for a few minutes, I'd call and there she'd be, just rolling her back on something on the ground. It was either something dead or some other critter's poop. Doggy perfume! A bath was usually called for after such outings.

Eventually, I had to get remote-control shock collars for all three. They were being a bit hardheaded about coming when we called them back from whatever they were chasing on the trails. One time, Tobey took off on the trail after a deer and ignored my calls, which terrified me. I was so afraid he'd end up on a highway or some hunter would shoot him. He came back on his own, but only after he was worn out and the deer had gotten away. The shock collars worked great—they listen now. We call, and if they ignore, we beep; if they still ignore, we zap. Tobey quickly became very good about coming when called, even better than anyone else. Junior remained slow about it; Dixie doodled along (they'd both take shortcuts off the trail to the truck where their treats were); and Hannah would come after a couple of calls—she usually had her nose to the ground tracking something, and my calls were not as important as what she was tracking. Tobey now actually waits and looks back at me for direction on the trails, and I'll point which way to go or say "this way," and the others follow Tobey in that direction.

The trails were especially great when the hay fields had tall grass waiting to be cut. We keep the trails clipped, so it's like walking in a park. There are so many different smells back there, and an abundance of all kinds of wildlife: squirrels to chase, turtles to fetch, turkeys and deer to spook and maybe chase. And skunks!

We had a skunk year. One afternoon, the dogs were a ways ahead of me on the trail. I couldn't see them around the bend, but I heard some commotion. I ran to where they were. Tobey had gotten a skunk. It must have been right on the trail when he saw it (go figure), and skunks don't run very fast! I yelled, "STOP! GET AWAY!" It was still alive and spraying. All the dogs got hit—mainly Tobey. I couldn't believe how strong the smell was; it was so strong it didn't even smell like skunk. After that, I had to put them in the dog truck to get them home for a bath. I tried everything I had in the house to wash them with. (I didn't have any tomato juice; you would have thought I'd have learned to keep a supply!) I used vinegar and liquid detergent, but nothing seemed to work. For the next six months, Tobey would get in the bed at night and lay his head next to mine on the pillow, and the smell of skunk would be in my face. I even bought a concoction called Skunk-Off from the pet store—that didn't work either.

The others lost the scent sooner, but our whole house smelled like skunk for at least a week. I burned scented candles and sprayed deodorizing spray of all kinds. It was awful. And then, after I thought the smell was getting fainter, I came back to the house from the barn, where I had been working horses one fall afternoon, to find a dead skunk in the front yard! That started another round of baths and Skunk-Off.

The dogs loved their treats. Usually they expected one after their dinner, while we were eating ours. They expected to eat when we did. Dixie would go up to the treat basket that sits on an antique sewing machine at the back door and stand and stare. If I didn't react, she'd turn her head and look back at me for a brief second and look back at the treats (like, "Didn't you see me here—don't you know what I want?"). I'd usually give in and give her a treat. If she'd already had two that evening, I'd say "That's all," and she'd go lie down. All the dogs knew exactly what we said; I'd been talking to them since they were born.

Tobey's technique was a little different. He'd go to the back door like he wanted to go out. Then, when I opened the door to let him out, he'd back up and look at the treat basket. I'd sneak him a treat—or try to—and he'd take it outside to eat so no one else would see him. Of course, they could hear so well—the rattle of a bag or box—it didn't take much for everyone else to jump up to ask, "If he got one, where's mine?" Hannah could be a bit picky about what kind of treat she had a taste for—Tobey, too, sometimes. When Hannah went to the treat basket, she had a specific treat in mind, and if I pulled one out that she wasn't interested in, she would actually shake her head "no." I'd pull out one after another, and I'd get the "no" shake until I got it right! A little spoiled, are we?

The dogs would always wait in the dog truck while we fed the horses, knowing that they would have a chance to play. They were so patient. In the summer, we planted a garden at the new barn because it was a sunnier place and we didn't have to worry about the pups eating our tomatoes. We tried planting some in pots at the house, and none ever made it to ripening. I think Dixie and Hannah were the culprits. They were the ones who followed me outside to get their "salad" when I threw lettuce and other vegetable cuttings in the woods. But I found I had to be careful picking any vegetables from the garden to take home in the dog truck as well. If I put them on the dash, they never made it home. I had to be careful with plastic cat food bowls, too. We have five barn cats, three at the new barn and two at the old barn. The cat food was stored at the new barn where we would fix two bowls of food twice a day for the old barn cats and drive over in the dog truck to feed them. Dixie mutilated several of the empty bowls that were inadvertently left on the dashboard.

*Tobey and Dixie sharing the passenger seat in the dog truck*

*Waiting to chase snowballs—Hannah, Junior, Dixie and Tobey*

*Romping in the snow, looking for snowballs*

*They loved exploring on the horseback riding trails.*

Dixie and Tobey were so close, but they communicated to us in different ways. Dixie always "talked" with her paws. She would use her front paws to pull her food bowl to her, hold onto a bone she was chewing, or toss a ball up in the air. When she wanted to come into the house, she would scratch the doors with her paw. I had heard somewhere that dogs can be taught to ring a bell to announce when they want to enter or leave their owner's house. So I sewed some huge jingle bells onto decorative tape to hang from the front and back doorknobs, in an effort to keep Dixie from tearing up the wooden doors. I thought that if she realized she could ring a bell to come in or go out, she might do that instead of scratching the doors. Well, that didn't work.

If Dixie wanted your attention or a treat, she would take that front paw and paw your leg with it. That was tolerable in the winter, but less so when you wore shorts in the summer.

Tobey, on the other hand, is a talker. He barks when he wants to come in the house, and communicates how anxious he is by the pitch of the bark. He'll moan or groan to communicate as well. He is very vocal about his needs. He has recently started pawing my leg, usually to remind me it's dinner time or that he wants a treat or an outing in the dog truck. Tobey acts as the protector of the other dogs: he goes around and cleans everyone's ears, checks on any boo-boos, cares for them with licks. But he'll still push everyone out of the way to get his treat first.

Some people don't notice, but every dog has its own way of wagging its tail. Dixie would get so excited, her whole back end wagged; Junior has a thumping wag, hitting anything in the way with great force; Tobey sometimes has a propeller wag, his tail going around in circles; and Hannah has a subtle wag, because she is so genteel and sweet!

*Dixie and Tobey, perfect siblings, knowing each other's moves*

# 12

## *Reuben*

In January 2012, around the end of the month, all of a sudden (as things usually happen), Junior wasn't feeling well. He was lethargic and didn't want to run with the others, hanging back when we were running in the field. He acted uncomfortable lying down.

I took him to see Dr. Bill. Bill was not in that afternoon, but the substitute doctor was very nice. They did an X-ray and found a six-inch piece of pig wire one-quarter inch in diameter under his skin near his stomach. Pig wire was used as fencing around parts of our farm; it's a smooth wire welded into four-inch squares. It is awful to get up, particularly after rusting. The doctor couldn't find any entry wound and said it could have entered through the skin several weeks ago and traveled through his body. We were lucky it hadn't punctured an organ. He did outpatient surgery and removed it during that visit. Thankfully, no damage was done, and Junior was back to normal in no time.

I've mentioned that Junior was a turtle dog and that he liked to carry things around in his mouth. Easter of 2013, Junior brought us a present. Around 2 a.m. (like I said, I'm a light sleeper), the dogs got me out of bed to let them out. Tobey and Junior went out. Tobey squeaked to come back in around 2:30, and Junior came in with him. Junior kept wandering around in the dark, so I asked him to get on his bed. I heard a little squeak, but didn't really think much of it.

At 4 a.m., I was catapulted out of bed by an awful squealing! Randy and I frantically tried to find the closest light to see what in the world was making such a racket. That's when I found a baby rabbit flailing around on the floor. I picked him up, got a towel, and dried him off. Junior had carried him around in his mouth without hurting him (of course, the bunny was in shock), and had dropped him when I told him to get into bed. I wasn't sure what to do with him. Deciding to go into the other bedroom, I wrapped him in a towel to keep him warm and held him against my chest, where he could hear my heartbeat.

Of course, I couldn't fall back asleep, worried that I might squash him. He was so tiny, and had probably just recently gotten his eyes open. I had raised baby wild rabbits before, and had always released them when they were old enough to fend for themselves. When trying to save my first baby rabbit, I received veterinarian instructions to feed it cow's milk mixed with a little sugar.

After not being able to fall back to sleep, I got up around 5:30. We didn't have much milk in the house. What we did have I worked with, and gave the little rabbit an eyedropper's-worth that morning. I had to go to work that day, so I planned to pick up milk and half-and-half at the grocery before returning home.

I placed him in a cardboard box with towels, hoping he'd recuperate from his shock. The first thing I did when I got home was feed him a combination of milk, half-and-half, and sugar with the eyedropper. I did this every three hours, even getting up twice in the middle of the night. One thing I know about babies: they need to eat often.

We named the rabbit "Reuben," because he was almost a sandwich! He was a feisty little rabbit. He started jumping out of his cardboard box after a week and a half. One morning I went in to feed him, and he wasn't anywhere in sight. The first time he'd jumped out, he was just on the bed where I had stationed the box; this time I couldn't find him anywhere. Randy came in to help and suggested looking behind the dresser; there he was, hiding. I guess he'd outgrown that cardboard box. He graduated to a cat carrier. I put a smaller cardboard box with towels in it for his hutch. He was just the cutest thing and would eat from that eyedropper really well for me. When he got enough to eat, he'd curl his nose and shake his head.

*Tiny Reuben*

If someone else entered the room while I was feeding him, Reuben would stop eating and sit very still in my hand. After about three weeks, I started putting clover in his box, then adding kale. I found out he loved dandelion flowers. I don't know what's in those, but he would jump up on top of his hutch box, jump off, run around his cage, and be really energetic after he had eaten some.

Reuben started chewing and biting on the metal grids of the carrier's door. He made sure I was in the room when he did that. He may have been trying to tell me something. If I put my hand in to catch him, he'd stand up on his hind legs and fight me with his front feet. Like I said, he was a feisty rabbit. I figured if he'd stand up to me, then he could take up for himself in the wild. Wild rabbits are not like domestic rabbits. They have survival instincts and do not respond the same way to affection as their domestic counterparts. I still knew he loved me, though. He responded to my voice and would come out of his hutch when I brought his meals. Being that he was so intent on biting his way out of the smaller townhouse, I decided to build him a condo by a stream downhill from the old barn, away from the cats and dogs. Randy took the building materials down in the front-end loader of the tractor. It was a six-foot-long tunnel-type rabbit condo with a rosebush at the back end, and I gathered sticks and limbs to camouflage the front entrance so he could hide and be safe.

One sunny day, after making sure it wasn't going to rain later (we'd had so much rain that spring), I took Reuben in his carrier, put the carrier in the back of my van, drove up to the old barn,

*Reuben on top of his "man-cave"*

*Reuben safe inside his hutch*

climbed over the fence, and walked down the hill and through the barbed-wire fence to his new condo. Positioning the carrier in front of his new home, I opened the door, thinking he would just hop out, so excited. Nothing. I sat beside the carrier for about fifteen minutes, trying to be patient, thinking he would at least be curious. Eventually I tipped the carrier up and dumped him out. He sat quietly for a few seconds, then ran back into his carrier. I guess he wasn't ready. So we packed up, walked up the hill to the car, and I took him home.

Considering another method to introduce him back into the wild, I built him a playpen of black netting (left over from covering our fish pond in the winter) staked with plastic removable fence posts, making an enclosure about four feet in diameter beside our driveway, just past the invisible dog fence. I put the carrier inside his playpen and secure the door open. The first day he did not come out. After two hours, I brought him home. The second time,

I dumped him out and he became curious and ate a little grass; but he didn't go too far from the carrier, so I brought him home after a couple of hours of "play" time. The third time, I had to chase him back into the carrier. I guess he was ready. So one sunny Saturday morning, I walked him down to his new condo, opened the carrier door and left. When I went back that afternoon to check on Reuben, he was gone.

*Reuben's townhouse, built by a novice rabbit condo contractor (me)*

That was June 8<sup>th</sup>. I believe we see him beside our driveway sometimes. These sightings were fairly frequent at first. I'd stop and say his name, and he would sit just inside the wood line and look at me. I think he recognizes my voice. We've also spotted two more rabbits hanging out near the same spot. They are a bit bigger than Reuben. I'm glad other rabbits are nearby to teach him rabbit things.

# 13

## Dixie's Challenge

It started this past spring, around the end of March 2013. Dixie started limping on her front leg. The limping would subside after she'd been on it for a while. At first, if she'd been napping on the sofa, woke up and jumped down, she would favor her front left leg. Then she started limping when we went for our run on the trails. Since she was only five-and-a-half years old, I figured she'd probably hurt it running or playing. Hannah had developed some arthritis in her back and had been prescribed Novox, an anti-inflammatory, so I started giving Dixie one of those pills each day. That seemed to help for a while, but then it became noticeable that she was limping all the time. I made an appointment to see Dr. Bill. He did an X-ray. It showed a bone cancer tumor above the elbow.

I was devastated, thinking it must be a mistake. I could scarcely believe what I was hearing. Bill went on to say that bone cancer has a tendency to migrate to the lungs. He took an X-ray of the chest and there was no indication of cancer. It was a good sign that we had caught it in time. He recommended that we make an appointment with a surgeon, because in most such cases, the leg had to be amputated.

I was torn about how she'd do with three legs. She seemed so much heavier in the front, and her back legs were a bit bowed. She also counted on using that front paw to communicate with us: scratching to come in the house, pawing me for attention or treats, holding a bone with both front paws to chew on it. When I got home after that first appointment with Bill, I went online and Googled "bone cancer in dogs." I found a site that offered a nutritional supplement that was supposed to help the immune system and portrayed stories of dogs with bone cancer who'd had limbs amputated and lived their normal lifespan of at least ten years. In most of these cases, the dogs were older when they were diagnosed with cancer. Dixie being only five years old, I had hope. When I called to order the nutritional supplements (I was up for anything that would help, and I didn't care how much it cost), the girl taking the order mentioned that Dixie shouldn't have dog food with any type of grain in it. Grain introduces sugar to the system and feeds the cancer cells. I immediately called Randy, who was out doing jobs, and asked him to go to the pet store and ask for grain-free dog food. She started her new diet that night. We also started feeding her kale (which she loved), shiitake mushrooms (which she could take or leave), carrots, and broccoli (which she has always loved), along with venison, roast beef, and chicken. We included any food or vitamin supplement that was known to help one's immune system and fight cancer.

It took a week to get an appointment with the surgeon. He was so nice. He explained that it might not be bone cancer; it could be one of four diseases, most of which would still require amputation. The recommendation was to take a biopsy to determine what type of cancer it was or whether it was cancer at all. The biopsy was scheduled for Wednesday, May 8th. I had to leave Dixie at the clinic that morning and go back and pick her up later. The surgeon assured me that they would get the biopsy results back by Friday of that week. Monday came and no word from the clinic. On Tuesday, I called—nothing. Wednesday, I called—they had not gotten the results. By Friday, I was really upset and called the clinic with an attitude. Finally, I talked to an associate who was really nice and helpful. She knew I was beside myself with frustration, and she called the pathologists and had the results within an hour.

Most dog lovers have heard that one year of human life equals seven years for a dog. I don't know who did those calculations, but if you break it down accordingly, one month would equal 213 days, one week would equal 53 days and one of our days would equal 7.5 dog days. When your baby has an aggressive cancer, those time calculations are important!

The diagnosis had taken so long because there was some question as to exactly what type of cancer it was. Three pathologists determined it was osteosarcoma. The surgery to amputate Dixie's leg was scheduled for Monday, May 20th. During the time it took for the three pathologists to make a diagnosis, her leg started really hurting her. She would lie on the floor at night and just whimper from the pain. It was tearing me apart. I would lie down beside her on a blanket, trying to console her, letting her know she was not alone. Bill had prescribed gabapentin and tramadol for the pain. I gave her as much pain medication as I could without over-medicating. Even with the medication, I spent a sleepless Friday night worrying and listening to her whimper.

By Saturday morning, she seemed a little better. She never lost her appetite, which enabled me to give her pills wrapped in some goody, such as ham. Come late afternoon, she was in extreme pain. I called the surgery clinic. She was scheduled for the amputation on Monday, but with the pain her leg was causing her, I wanted it off as soon as possible. They said to bring her in to the emergency care clinic so that they could give her an IV for the pain.

We were distraught. Randy brought the car around to the back door so she wouldn't have as far to walk. He was so upset that he hit a tree in the process and dented the side of the car.

I crawled in the back to ride with her. Her whimpering was making me ache for her. She had never whimpered about anything before. She was so brave: she went right on inside the clinic with us. The pain injections helped tremendously. They also recommended a prescription for morphine tablets and sent her back home with us. Saturday night, she seemed better after we got home. But by 4 a.m. Sunday, I heard her whimpering again. By 5:30 a.m., we had her back in the car and I drove her as fast as I could to the ER. They kept her that time with IV pain meds. Her surgery finally happened on Monday, May 20th.

I was relieved now that the leg was gone. In hindsight, we probably should have done that instead of waiting on the biopsy. The surgeon was so good about calling us and Bill about the results. He called in the early afternoon and said she'd done excellently— the leg had actually broken at the site of the tumor, and the lymph glands and lungs were clear of disease according to the X-rays. We were on the road to recovery.

## 14

## *Dixie's Bravery*

Next step: chemo. I was ready for her to start chemotherapy at the time of the surgery, but the oncologist believed that her body needed to expel any anesthesia or drug residue and recover from the stress of surgery first. That sounded logical. We had to wait two weeks, and an appointment was made to remove her staples from surgery.

What a brave girl. Everyone in the clinic loved her. She was so sweet and would wag her tail at everyone and give kisses. The surgeon said she recovered quicker than any amputee he'd ever

*Keeping my girl company after surgery*

had. She was up and hopping around that morning and went outside to do her business and was back to her happy self. She was ready to leave the next day.

I was amazed at how well she got along with three legs; she would hop and her ears would flap up and down with each hop—so adorable. Dogs are amazing at adapting to situations.

She seemed back to normal except for missing that leg. Her appetite was good and she wanted to go up to the barn in the dog truck. One of our exercise step boxes from the basement was perfect to put in front of the side doors to help her get in and out of the truck. We still had to watch that the other dogs wouldn't knock her over. In about a week, it was hard for me to keep up with her on the trail. I was so uplifted by how well she was doing.

*Side by side as always. I think he is worrying over her.*

*Group session in the hall*

*Asking momma for advice*

*Missing a leg doesn't affect the nose*

*Happily exploring*

*Same as always, ready to jump out of the truck*

*Dixie in the passenger seat, still using the armrest*

*Dixie relaxing in my lap after her amputation*

*Not feeling like a romp in the field today*

The plan was to give her two different chemo drugs for six treatments, alternating the drugs. Both drugs were approved to treat osteosarcoma. We didn't know how her body would react to chemo, but the oncologist reassured us that she would prescribe medication for any adverse reactions to the drugs. You would not have known she'd had any chemo at all; there were no outward side effects.

She would still get in the bed to sleep with us at night. It took a couple of nights for her to figure out how to redistribute her weight so she could sleep on her back with three legs. She would also get in the passenger seat of the dog truck and put that good leg up on the armrest, just like always. We just knew she could beat this disease and be in that 20 percent of dogs who go into total remission—she was too young not to.

We wanted to be with her as much as possible, so we took her for a trip to visit Jim and Marie and Chelsea on the Bay. I think she really enjoyed the one-on-one attention. We had to keep a close eye on her, though: she went down to the pier like she really wanted to jump off into the water! We had not purchased a life vest yet. We were hoping to get one for her so she could continue to enjoy her favorite sport. We had a great visit.

Dixie had to have blood work (CBC) done once a week between the chemo treatments. We'd take her to see Dr. Bill for that (she liked going to his clinic more than the clinic where she was getting chemo treatments). All the blood tests came back looking good. We were optimistic. On the second trip for her chemo, I was sitting in the waiting area, talking to another patient's owner. She said that her Australian greyhound had been diagnosed with a tumor and given only six weeks to live. He was fourteen years old and was still doing well after eighteen months of treatment. I was really encouraged by that.

On our third trip to the oncologist, she found a tumor above Dixie's amputation site between the shoulder and the neck, about the size of a small peach. The doctor took a smear and found it cancerous, but it was a different type of cancer—not osteosarcoma. The chemo drugs were not working. This new (if it was indeed new) cancer could be melanoma or another type of cancer that affected blood cells. If that were the case, Dixie would need to be put on a different chemo drug. The doctor was going to send a tissue sample to Cornell University for diagnosis.

Instead of waiting another week (or 53 dog days) for that diagnosis, the doctor administered another chemo drug right then in hopes that it would fight this new cancer. We switched things up and changed some of her medication and were to visit in another two weeks with CBC blood work in between. At the oncologist visits, Dixie had gotten so she didn't want to go to the back rooms of the clinic with the assistants, and would look at me as if to say, "I don't want to leave you." I guess any mother would be torn, wanting to keep her baby with her, but knowing she needed to go for her own good. Dixie was so brave. I started taking chicken jerky treats in with me to give to the assistants, so that they could coax her into the back operatories with them.

All the blood work between chemo treatments looked good. On our next chemo visit, they were going to take chest X-rays and the test results from Cornell would be in.

That's when this book started:

August 15, 2013

Dixie did really well today; she acted like she felt good. The prednisone has brought her appetite back to where it was before she became ill, which means she will enthusiastically eat her bowl of food and then look for more. She actually hopped all the way to the pond from the new barn on our outing this morning. She was interested in exploring what the other dogs found interesting down there. She had to stop several times going back up the hill. Her breathing seemed labored. The tumor above the amputated leg is still growing; it's about the size of an orange.

August 18, 2013

Dixie no longer cares to go to the barn in the mornings. She'll go in the afternoon and will get out of the van with everyone, do some sniffing, and go short distances. She tires out really fast. She's been coughing some, too, which makes me think the lesions in her lungs are depriving her of oxygen.

August 19, 2013

Dixie woke me around 1:30 a.m., panting. She was having trouble getting comfortable on the floor. I turned the overhead fan on to add to the fan on the floor. About 2 a.m., she decided to get in the bed. She has always slept with us, loves to cuddle and be close, but she hasn't done that for the last two weeks; she just gets too hot now. The weather has been cool and rainy the last couple of days, but I guess she was still uncomfortable, because after a while, she got back down on the floor. I gave her an additional prednisone and tramadol. Around 4:30 or 5 a.m., she seemed to be breathing a bit better. I'm not supposed to give her additional medications according to the oncologist, but at this point, I'll do anything to make her more comfortable. I'm in such a terrible dilemma: I can't bear for her to suffer and don't know how I'm going to bear to have her put to sleep.

Later this morning, her appetite is still good. Thank the Lord, or she wouldn't be getting her medicine wrapped in a ham slice. She also likes the canned pumpkin recommended for fiber for her digestion. She also loves her chicken and still enjoys those treats. She ate her breakfast and seemed a bit better. She still has labored breathing and is panting excessively. Dixie did decide, after some coaxing, to go to the barn with us, so we went to the front field in front of the farmhouse. We had cut some trails throughout the perimeter of that field and around the trees while we were waiting for the hay to be cut, so we would have a place for the dogs to explore. I pulled the step box out for her and she got out of the truck, but she didn't seem interested in exploring. I stayed back with her, letting the others go around sniffing. Next thing I knew, she was back in the truck, waiting for her treat. I gave her one and sat on the side of the truck, hugging her. After letting the others explore a while, I gathered everyone back into the truck to go home.

August 19, 2013

In the afternoon, I called Bill to order some antibiotics for Hannah. She has skin lesions or dermatitis that will clear up if she is on an antibiotic for a short time. I asked him if there was something we could give Dixie to help with her breathing and lung function. He did know of a drug that would help open her airways, and called in a prescription for us. We're so excited for the hope. We picked up the new prescription this afternoon and started it right away. This evening, I stayed up with her, lying beside her on the floor, stroking her, hoping to relax her so her breathing wouldn't be so labored. The tumor is about the size of a grapefruit now.

August 20, 2013

Dixie ate her breakfast along with her medications and went outside with the others. She doesn't feel as good today. She didn't want to get in the dog truck with us to go to the barn. She came into the house and lay in the hall in front of the fan all day, just panting. This evening, I lay on the floor with her most of the night, waiting for her to fall asleep. She was panting so hard she couldn't sleep. I gave her more of the medications; it didn't help.

August 21, 2013

Around 4 a.m., I decided to lie down in the bed for a bit. At 5 a.m. (she is so good), she came in to wake me to let her outside. She hopped right out the door to the woods to do her business. She is such a good girl. She didn't come directly back from the woods, though. I took a flashlight out to check on her and found her lying behind the hot tub where the damp ground was cool. I let her stay where she was. At 6:30 a.m., she had moved next to the water bucket. I took more medications wrapped in a ham slice out to her and she ate that. At 7:30 a.m., I took breakfast out to her beside the water bucket, but she wouldn't eat. Later I took her water bowl out to her with ice in it, and she drank a lot of water. I hooked the fan up to the outlet at the back door so that it would blow on her while she was lying outside. It's going to be a hot one today. I had called Bill to make her an appointment this morning, hoping we could find something to help with the panting. He wouldn't be in the office until 3 p.m. She just keeps panting so hard, she can't relax or sleep. She really feels bad. She will still wag her tail a couple of times when we go out to stroke and love on her, but not like usual.

At 11:45 a.m., she decided that it was too hot outside and came in to be in front of the air conditioner and fan.

It's so hard to let go, but when you know they are struggling and uncomfortable, it's time to do the kindest and most loving thing you can do.

At 2:20 p.m., we got all the other dogs inside the house. Dixie had gone outside and was lying on the damp ground again. I opened the side doors of the van and she surprised me by jumping in. She was a little weak on her hind legs, but I think she enjoys the ride. She wouldn't eat her treat when she got in the van like she usually does. We had a 3 p.m. appointment to see Bill. The girls at the clinic had asked me to come inside to make sure the waiting room was free of other patients before bringing Dixie into the office. Faye came out with me to help get Dixie out of the van. Dixie usually just jumps out, but this time she didn't want to come. In the course of that short drive, she had gotten weak. Faye had to help me lift her out of the van. She made it into the office, but immediately slumped down on the floor just inside the door. We were able to maneuver her onto the weight scales. Then it took two associates and me with a harness under her stomach to get her into the exam room. This is the first day she hasn't wanted to eat. While talking with Bill this morning, he said not to give her the prednisone today. He thinks that the prednisone might be making her pant excessively. Her liver has enlarged—probably due to the prednisone as well. She's only been on it one-and-a-half weeks. He started talking about changing her medications to try to keep her from panting so hard. We are still on that roller-coaster ride—having hope again that she could feel better.

You would think that after four months of ups and downs with her illness, I would have accepted the fact that she wasn't going to beat this thing. I sat on the exam room floor beside her, stroking her head and talking to her, hoping to comfort her in some way, not being able to control my tears. She is so brave and has such a happy heart. I left it up to her: I said, "Dixie, do you want to go home? Let's go get in the truck." We opened the exam room door like we were leaving, but she just lay her head down on her paws. She was so tired.

I stayed for the first shot, a sedative. Finally, she relaxed and stopped panting and went to sleep while I was rubbing her head and back. I couldn't stay for the lethal dose. I was crying too hard, the tears blinding me, causing me to back into a shrub in the clinic parking lot.

# 15

## *The Hole in My Heart*

August 21, 2013

A I just can't stop sobbing. I am so unbelievably sad. I was angry with God when we lost Momma to cancer at the age of sixty-six (entirely too young), because He is the ultimate and responsible for humans. Momma did everything the doctors told her to do. She had gone through radiation, surgery, and chemo. Nothing worked for her either. With Dixie I'm not angry with God; I'm just so indescribably sad. Was I too ignorant to prevent her cancer? We're the ones responsible for our pets' health.

It's so sad that she won't continue to have the same happy outings as her siblings. It would be easier to accept if she had been older. She was such a happy girl: sensitive, so loving, and thoughtful at times. Her love showed through her tail wags (actually her whole rear end would wag), her kisses, and her smiles.

People who love their pets always wonder if they will be waiting for them in heaven. I heard a lay minister speak once who said the Bible states that your pets will be in heaven waiting for you. Another was quoted as saying, "It wouldn't be heaven for you without your beloved pets."

September 6, 2013

I brought Dixie home today. I knew that the veterinary clinic would have to be the last stop of the day. I couldn't talk or think about it without sobbing. I didn't tell Randy that she was ready to come home; he had special race plans with friends and I didn't want him thinking about it. I cried off and on all day, missing my baby girl. I can't seem to stop grieving. I miss her so terribly!

When I got home, Tobey of course ran to the dog truck for his afternoon outing. I unloaded groceries and dog treats, changed my clothes, and opened the doors to the truck for all to get in. After closing the doors to the truck, I went back to my van and brought Dixie's urn into the house. Then I took Hannah, Junior, and Tobey for a run on the trails.

I wanted to get everything done—my paperwork and the dogs' dinners—so I could concentrate on making a special place for Dixie. I cleaned the area around the pie safe where Jake's urn is displayed. Dixie's urn is a really pretty one: bronze with puppy feet as the base (since she lost one of hers).

There's a huge hole in my heart that will never stop hurting, a hole dedicated to my "baby-girl-Doodle." I just can't believe she's gone. There's not a day that goes by that I haven't cried; everything reminds me of her. Sometimes I just break down and sob. Sometimes I fight back tears. Sometimes I just wail. I miss her so terribly, and all my daily routines remind me of our loss—that she's not here with us—taking the others out for their romp in the fields, sleeping in the bed and not having her curled up by my legs. I knew it was going to be hard losing one. But I never expected that we would have to deal with it this soon.

I am so emotionally attached to animals. I just want to take care of them, love them, and make them happy.

Tobey still has his crown jewels. We're in hopes of one day finding him a suitable mate (I know he wants one). This time, we would probably be getting the pick of the litter, rather than helping the momma raise them. That was a once-in-a-lifetime experience.

*Dixie and Jake, immortal in our hearts*

# Epilogue
## *My Hero*

The thought never crossed my mind that I would be writing this chapter.

January 23, 2015

We lost Tobey today. I feel like I've been kicked in the ribs by a 1,200-pound horse, knocking all the breath out of me. Upon waking, the numbness set in. All our hopes of continuing Jake's legacy have been dashed and I just can't believe that he is gone, my baby boy, my joy.

It has been a tough two months. I had been worried about him during August and September. He didn't seem to have his usual energy and would limp some on his left front leg. After losing Dixie only a year ago, I became a worrywart about any abnormalities and wanted to make sure we were proactive about any health issues. We scheduled an appointment for an exam and bloodwork. This showed no abnormalities, but as a precaution, Bill prescribed an antibiotic in case the symptoms were due to a disease acquired from a tick bite. Tobey seemed to feel better after that treatment for a couple of weeks. Then he started limping on his right front leg. We went back to see Dr. Bill for more blood work and X-rays of the limbs; at least we would have those records to compare to any future lab work or X-rays.

During the month of November, he became really picky about his food. He was still excited about the chicken jerky and duck jerky treats when he got back in the dog truck from our trail walks, but we had to really dress up his meals for him to eat. He had really slowed down, and was the last one back to the truck when we went on our outings. I noticed he had some diarrhea and occasionally would dry heave. On Friday, December 5th, another appointment was made for more blood work and an exam; at this time, Bill took a sample of an enlarged lymph gland. We got a call from Bill on Monday, the 8th. The results came back as lymphoma. I couldn't believe that this could happen to us again. I collapsed on my knees beside my bed and sobbed.

We were assured that lymphoma in dogs is one of the cancers that reacts well to chemotherapy, and statistics showed that the chances were good that he could maintain a good quality of life for two years or more. Labs were one of the breeds that seem to do well with this therapy. There was that hope again.

Lucky, the oncologist had an opening Wednesday the 10th, and we went in for Tobey's first chemo treatment. He seemed to feel so much better after that. His lymph glands had diminished in size; we were so excited that he could be on the road to recovery.

The protocol for lymphoma was for Tobey to receive a different chemo drug every week for at least four weeks, and then every other week. The total treatment program was scheduled out for twenty-five weeks. Of course, since the first treatment made him feel better, we went back in the next week for his second treatment. He had an unexpected adverse reaction to this drug; it attacked his gastrointestinal tract and made him deathly ill. We rushed him back to oncology the next day. He was dehydrated and would have died if IV fluids had not been administered. The oncologist said this had never happened before and was so surprised by such an adverse reaction. She did say that due to some genetic throwback to the wolf, such as in the collie breed, cases of this drug reaction had been documented, but normally not this quickly. She was so apologetic—it's all a crapshoot.

The oncology clinic is closed on Friday, so we went to Bill's for IV fluids all day Friday. It seemed the fluids would leak out of him as fast as they were administered. My boy was so miserable. Back to Bill's on Saturday for more fluids; this time they seemed to stay in him and he seemed to feel better. Bill prescribed several medications for nausea and to increase his appetite. During phone conversations with the oncologist, she agreed that Tobey needed time to get over the past chemo treatment before starting any other treatment, and that this could take several weeks.

To help stimulate his appetite, I cooked fresh venison. He really liked that the first day, but not the next.

I bought special meals at the pet store, which he seemed to like one day, but not another. KFC extra-crispy fried chicken he liked one day, but not the next. Finally, after three weeks, he did start doing better, and his digestion seemed almost normal. On Monday the 12th, we went back to the oncologist for bloodwork and an exam. His lymph glands were still swollen. She suggested starting over with the first chemo drug. It had been four weeks since he'd had that drug and he did do well with it.

He didn't regain that Tobey energy like the first time, though. He still wanted to get in the dog truck for our outings and he came down to the basement when I was exercising to play tug-of-war. In playing and wrestling with him, I noticed there was significant swelling in his groin area, and I immediately ran upstairs to call Bill.

Randy took him in for Bill to do an exam on Friday, January 16th. This time the chemo treatment didn't work. It was the lymphoma causing the swelling. We already had an appointment scheduled for the following Monday with oncology. Tobey had not eaten anything significant since that previous Saturday. During this appointment, it was suggested that we give him steroids, which usually has an effect on swollen lymph glands; and subcutaneous fluids; plus another chemo drug that was supposed to have little or no side effects on the gastrointestinal track.

By Wednesday, he was even sicker. I didn't know what to do. I couldn't bear to see him feeling so bad. Dr. Bill was out of town this week on a much-needed vacation. He never takes a vacation! I was an emotional basket case. Back to oncology: this time they admitted him to the emergency clinic for fluids, steroids, and nutritional support. This was an overnight stay. Tobey had never stayed overnight anywhere before.

The oncologist thought the steroids would give us at least two weeks of quality time. They were wrong again.

I picked him up around mid-day on Thursday. He wagged his tail at seeing me, but wouldn't be coaxed into eating anything. The emergency clinic said he'd eaten a little bit Wednesday night, but he would have nothing to do with food now. I also had to help him into the van to come home: there was significant swelling along both sides of his chest and abdomen.

When we got home he got out of the van and went into the woods. He had a lot of fluid to release. Tobey didn't seem interested in coming into the house. He would wander around in the woods, digging at the earth and looking for a cool place to bed down.

Friday morning at 2 a.m., he woke me. I could tell he was feeling bad and wanted to go out. At 3 a.m., I got dressed and went outside in a panic, looking and calling for him. I called and called and finally my good man came up to the backyard. He wagged his tail at seeing me and came back in the house. During the day on Friday, we would find him down by the edge of the driveway where the invisible fence stopped, and we'd go down and coax him back toward the house. He would wander around in the woods like he was looking for something.

When I was growing up, most dogs stayed outside, and my parents would say that dogs know when it is their time and will wander off to die. By Friday afternoon, Tobey had found a place in the leaves under a cedar tree near the tractor shed and made a bed. We couldn't get him to leave that bed. He wouldn't even raise his head. Touching his side caused him to wrench from the pain of his swollen glands.

It was starting to rain, so Randy and I put up a canopy tent to cover him, along with a blanket to keep him warm. We wanted someone we knew to come out to relieve his pain, so we called our equine vet. They were so good to come on short notice, and Tobey didn't have to be moved. We couldn't bear to see him suffer anymore.

The cremation company that took care of Jake, Dixie, and now Tobey was wonderful enough to come out and pick him up. It seems so unfair to lose both my dearest babies so close together. He now has Dixie to play with again. There will never be another Tobey or Dixie in my life; they were truly special.

The following was sent to us via e-mail; it is so beautiful, I wanted to share it:

*People are born so they can learn to live a good life, like loving everybody all the time and being nice, right? Well, dogs already know how to do that, so they don't have to stay as long.*
*If a dog were the teacher, you would learn things like:*
*When loved ones come home, always run to greet them.*
*Never pass up an opportunity to go for a joyride.*
*Allow the experience of fresh air and the wind in your face to be pure ecstasy.*
*Take naps.*

# My Hero

*Stretch before rising.*

*Run, romp, and play daily.*

*Thrive on attention and let people touch you.*

*Avoid biting when a simple growl will do.*

*On warm days, stop to lie on your back in the grass.*

*On hot days, drink lots of water and lie under a shady tree.*

*When you're happy, dance around and wag your entire body.*

*Delight in the simple joy of a long walk.*

*Be loyal.*

*Never pretend to be something you are not.*

*If what you want lies buried, dig until you find it.*

*When someone is having a bad day, be silent, sit close by, and nuzzle them gently.*

# Acknowledgments

Thanks especially to my cousin Bill (Dr. William Dunnavant of Ironbridge Animal Hospital), who was and is there for us whenever we have concerns regarding the health of our "babies." And thanks to his staff, who are like family as well.

Thanks to Dr. Roy Barnes, Dixie's surgeon, who was so caring and empathetic. Thanks also to Dr. Angharad Waite, our oncologist, who did all she could for Dixie.

I want to thank all of our Farm Family for their love and support and for covering the barn chores so I could get away to the beach to complete this book over Labor Day week in 2013.

Thanks to all our good friends and family who have expressed their sympathy for what we've been going through. And thanks to my sister Karen for her encouragement and the publisher leads she provided to me as I wrote this book, as well as to my cousin, Aleta, who guided me through her publisher to the kind people at Belle Isle Books.

And thank you, Randy, my wonderful husband, for going through all of this with me and being there for my emotional support, as well as putting up with all my wacky ideas!

I love all of you.

## About the Author

Gail Canada is a true farm girl, living on the same farm where she grew up. The farm is her soul and holds all her childhood memories. She and her husband, Randy, have turned the dairy farm into a horse-boarding facility. She started a window treatment installation business when women didn't really do that kind of manual work, and was fortunate to have Randy to assist in both operations.

Gail wrote a column called *The Groovy Guru* for her high school newspaper and excelled in journalism classes. This is her first book.

CPSIA information can be obtained
at www.ICGtesting.com
Printed in the USA
LVOW06s1425310316
481607LV00046B/262/P